Growing for Showing

GEORGE E. WHITEHEAD

Growing for Showing

With drawings by Anne Shingleton

FABER AND FABER
LONDON AND BOSTON

First published in 1978
by Faber and Faber Limited
3 Queen Square London WC1
Printed in Great Britain by
Latimer Trend & Company Ltd Plymouth
All rights reserved

British Library Cataloguing in Publication Data

Whitehead, George Edward
Growing for showing.
1. Vegetable gardening   2. Horticultural exhibitions
3. Fruit-culture   4. Horticultural exhibitions
I. Title
635   SB322
ISBN 0–571–11206–4

Contents

CONTENTS

Illustrations

Acknowledgements

I am very grateful to all those who have given me help in various ways: to Anne Shingleton for the line drawings; Pamela Harrington for the typing; Ron Oulds for the photograph on the back cover; and Jean Gay and my publishers for taking so much trouble over the preparation and production of the text.

Introduction

Throughout the years, between the two world wars and those that have passed since the last holocaust, most of my Saturdays through the months of August have been spent in judging or showing at town and country flower shows, such as are held throughout Britain at that season of the year. Quite often I have staged my own entries at the local event before dashing off to adjudicate elsewhere. Later in the day I return hopefully to collect my awards and dispose of the produce. These August Saturdays have been among the happiest days of my longish life.

Although the types of competitor have changed somewhat – the old spartan head gardeners being superseded by keen amateurs – the general pattern is much the same. There are the few who hog the cups and the prize money. There are also the hopeless optimists who never succeed and ever fail to learn. In between are the many very keen growers, both professional and amateur, who do not quite make the grade because they lack that additional know-how that will upset the champions. If you are in the last category the prime object of this book is to demonstrate to you how to grow, prepare and show what you produce in ways that will inspire confidence and, undoubtedly, bring certain success.

Very often I am asked by people who know that I write gardening columns, whether there are books upon this subject. My reply is that, as far as I know, there are none in circulation, although there have been works written in the past. They were compiled by experts, but not by people who took chances in open competition. In this respect I think I am unique.

I have mused over the idea for years, and many times considered the problems involved. For instance, should I reiterate all the usual information found in scores of general gardening books and journals and reiterated on the radio and television, or should I assume that the readers already have a certain amount of experience in gardening? If I gave the full rigmarole it would make an enormous tome. I decided to cut the usual advice, and to concentrate upon those essential additional treatments that make all the difference between the ordinary and the exceptional. Where recognised good cultivations cannot be improved upon, I have completely omitted any references to the growing methods. In other instances, where I think the requisite knowledge is unlikely to be found in general gardening books, I have gone into considerable detail.

While skilful growing techniques are often essential, the presentation of the finished produce is always of the utmost importance, therefore I have elaborated on this over and over again. Through the years I've seen thousands of exhibits that would have received high awards, but were unplaced through careless or faulty preparation and bad staging. It seems such a shame that growers will take months, even years, to grow first-class vegetables, fruit and flowers and then spoil their chances in the testing stages. Judges have to obey the rules, as do the entrants, and to make decisions upon what they see, and not as the produce was, although they do often give credit for what it is to be.

While this book is written primarily to help the general gardener succeed in the August flower shows, I am fully aware that there are events in other months, like the sweet pea and rose shows held in summer in many places. Then in

November there are the numerous chrysanthemum exhibitions. In most August flower shows there are classes for these flowers, but only to a minor degree when compared with those shows specially organised for them in their proper seasons. My notes regarding their cultivation and presentation are enough to help the August competitors, but if one is to compete in the specialised events, considerably more knowledge, time and expenditure, is needed.

I must mention that there are many organisations at either international, national, or local level that are limited to the exclusive promotion of a particular family, or section of a family, of plant life. Among these are societies for alpines, cacti, chrysanthemums, camellias, carnations, dahlias, delphiniums, ferns, fuchsias, gladioli, heaths, houseplants, irises, orchids, pelargoniums, roses, sweet peas and violas. Techniques of cultivation, lists and descriptions of the latest varieties, and reports of their shows are circulated among members. Should you aspire to become a specialist it is imperative to join up with such devotees of your favourite flower.

The advice I give here is, I repeat, intended to assist the general gardener to become a better all-round grower and shower, and to raise the standard of the general classes where he or she may compete. It is just possible that, by being successful in the local competitions, you may aspire to join the ranks of the specialists but I hope that not too many will do so. There is more fun in being the best all-rounder in the district. *If you take to heart what I have written you will be.*

I

The General Approach

Whether on an international, national, provincial or village level, every show is subject to a very carefully prepared schedule, its size depending upon the importance of the event. Therefore the first thing an aspiring competitor must do is to obtain a copy in order to determine to what extent he or she can participate.

Usually the village schedules are prepared by the organisers several months beforehand so that gardeners can grow their produce especially for this purpose. There are also other classes included in the schedule, for many skills, such as cookery, home-made wine, handicrafts, needlework etc etc. That is by the way.

Actually, although the annual event is invariably described as a 'Flower Show', flowers seldom dominate. Taking the schedule of the 'Society' of the village in which I live as an example, only 35 of the 200 classes are for cultivated flowers. There are others for floral art, but the majority are for vegetables and those other miscellaneous subjects just referred to.

The vegetable, fruit and flower classes are segregated into sections that should be heeded. In the case of my village, there are three categories: members' classes, parishioners' classes and 'open' classes. According to the rules, as I am a member *and* a parishioner I can enter in every class of the horticultural sections. If I were a member but not a parish-ioner, I could enter only in the first and third sections. It always pays to study the rules.

The next subject to consider is that of the challenge cups generally awarded to those competitors who collect most points according to the prizes won. Three points for a first, two for a second, and one for a third, are generally given, but in a few classes, notably collections, these are doubled, or trebled; therefore if you aspire to win any of these trophies you are spurred on to enter as many impressive classes as possible, either in a special section or for the complete championship.

A Special Plot

While you may be successful in many instances without practising special methods of cultivation, if you really want to become a champion you must grow many things exception-ally well, and the best way to do that is to reserve a part of the kitchen garden for the purpose. In it you will grow not only extraordinarily good vegetables, you will also cultivate some special flowers that demand an unusual degree of attention.

The first mistake the beginner makes in this regard is to devote too much space to exhibition-class subjects. You only need a few specimens of each. When I was in charge of large estate gardens I reserved a small plot for growing some of my show produce. This enabled me to increase its fertility as the years passed, and the quality of the vegetables and flowers grown therein improved year by year.

In my special plot were, in addition to many of the vegetables, some of the important flowers such as outdoor chrysanthemums, dahlias, China asters, and zinnias. But I did not grow certain vegetables and flowers such as sweet peas and gladioli in the reserved ground, for they need plenty of room and a frequent change of site.

Varieties

The next mistake the beginner makes is to try to impress the judges by growing and showing novelties. Judges mostly consist of professional gardeners or horticultural experts, who are somewhat conservative in their tastes and preferences. Only when a novelty is extraordinarily outstanding is it regarded favourably. A good rule is to never worry much about new varieties, but to concentrate upon growing ordinary varieties extraordinarily well.

Quality

The next mistake is that new competitors think size is paramount, so they enter the largest specimens regardless of evenness. One should always have in mind three points when selecting the actual specimens to be put on the bench; they are quality, evenness and then size. These are the three common virtues but often size can be a detriment. Hints about selecting the right blossoms to put in the vases or which vegetables on the dishes are discussed when we come to the various types.

Containers

Exhibits of flowers are so often ruined by having vases that topple over through being top-heavy and this is especially so with heavy subjects, such as six mighty stems of gladioli. Once an exhibit is damaged, the judges have little sympathy. They only judge as they see the exhibits, and not as they were, or will be, although they are sometimes inclined towards the latter state rather than the former. Once suitable containers have been obtained they can be used year after year. Although plastic vases are seen more often, they are not as practicable as the good old heavy earthenware containers which are sturdy and enhance, rather than detract from, the living things put into them.

Equipment

Old showmen generally carry a kit box in which is included a pair of sharp-pointed scissors, a stout pocket knife, labels, pencils, some raffia, a cloth or two, and a fine syringe. If they live near the venue, they might use buckets and cans in which to transport the flowers they are staging. Otherwise, the blooms are carefully packed in flat marketing boxes and secured in the same way that nurserymen send their carnations to market.

Siting

The experienced exhibitor makes a point of getting to the show as early as possible, not only to allow plenty of time to stage the various entries, but also to choose (if the rules permit) the best positions for the vegetables, fruit or flowers to be staged. In some shows, the places where you are to put your exhibits are marked and you must observe them. However, in others, spaces are merely allotted according to the number of entries and, if you are first to arrive, you can choose which you think is the most advantageous site for all your exhibits.

When I first enter the marquee, or building, I collect the show cards that have been written out for me for placing against each exhibit and then I walk round with them to put each one in the best-available spaces in the respective classes. To make doubly sure I also position the plates or containers to be used. Among competitors, this placing of the show card is generally regarded as a reservation for your entry.

When selecting a space I am guided by two factors. One is shading. In many marquees there are old and new roof covers, thus affecting the light. I visualise where the sun will be shining upon that roof at midday, which is about the time when the judges will be busy. If the venue is in a building, as is often the case nowadays, I notice the positioning of the windows.

The other point is, if possible, to reserve an end space of a class, especially if it is for a collection of perennials or dahlias, or vegetables. Which end is chosen depends upon the sun and shade position as mentioned in the last paragraph, or upon the subjects of the adjoining class. For example, if the end space of a class for asters is next to that of a class for dahlias, I avoid it, for the latter are likely to detract from the colours of my asters, especially if they are of a type that will clash. But if the adjoining class is of a less brilliant flower, or a less imposing one, I have only the neighbouring competitor in my own class to offset my display against. Watching colours and striving to arrange them so that those of your competitors enhance rather than detract from your own is fair and honest.

You are out to impress the judges and influence them in your favour, purely by what they see. Judges are honest men. They are also human. They always make their decisions without fear or favour. But they can be impressed, and first impressions most times last longest.

2

Principal Vegetables Considered

Seeing that vegetables are given priority in most flower show schedules, it is only fitting that we should deal with them first in these pages. They are the ultimate manifestation of a general gardener's skill, for to have the finest specimens at their peak of perfection on a certain day needs a lot of knowledge and demands an immense amount of work and many weeks of diligent attention.

I've often heard sour remarks made about the top-class vegetables displayed in shows, suggesting that they are too large or inedible when compared with those of inferior size. Actually, the reverse is the case. A large percentage of the content of vegetables is flavoured water, and if they are served without too much having been boiled out of them they are far superior to any grown in fields, or *badly* cultivated in gardens. They are definitely more tender and have better flavour if not fed with strong fertilisers, or frequently dressed with pesticides, as are commercial crops. Even those who verbally despise them, gratefully accept these wonderful vegetables when offered.

Emphasis is on quality and condition all the time. Coarseness and every sort of imperfection is frowned upon. Colour, freshness, and shapeliness are more important than size.

Most judges are influenced, if not completely guided, by *The Horticultural Show Handbook*, published by the Royal

Horticultural Society 'for the Guidance of Organisers, Schedule-Makers, Exhibitors and Judges' at general shows. If you take showing seriously, or contemplate becoming a judge, this book should be studied carefully. At the same time, it should not be taken to heart to such a degree that you follow it to the letter. The chief thing that it will do is reveal what judges look for regarding fruit and flowers as well as vegetables, by going into details of judging by various forms of marking.

Pointing

As an example, when judging carrots there should be a maximum of 5 points for condition, 3 points for form, 6 points for colour and 6 points for uniformity. I have yet to meet a judge who gets out his pencil and scrutinises carrots to that extent. It might be necessary if there were many entries of top quality, but I've yet to meet such a show.

These maximum points, totalling 20, are only given to carrots and the other first-class vegetables – cauliflowers, celery, leeks, onions, parsnips, peas and potatoes. If, therefore, you show a collection, the more you have of these kinds in your exhibit, the more chance you have of winning, providing that they are super specimens. Only the total points for each vegetable are revealed on the show cards, just to enable competitors to see where they stand with their rivals.

Runner beans can be given 8 points for condition, 3 for size, 3 for form, and 4 for uniformity, making 18 in all. Similarly, cucumbers and tomatoes are 18-pointers. After that several vegetables, including asparagus, dwarf beans, beet, cabbages, and turnips can be given a possible 15. Therefore it is hopeless to put these or other low-pointing vegetables into small collections.

Notwithstanding, I usually find that I can gain more points from well-grown runner beans and tomatoes in a collection than I can from parsnips or cauliflowers. This is because the judges are inclined to award easy points to the former two vegetables, marking down the latter for the slightest defects.

As far as points go in the separate dishes, apart from helping one decide which to include in a collection, it is best to ignore them altogether and select one's best of the various crops. In the succeeding chapters, I have described how to grow, prepare and stage them to the best of one's ability, and to do so with confidence.

Collections

A winning collection of vegetables is a triumph of skill, no matter whether it be for a small display in the village hall or marquee, or a comprehensive one such as is held in the RHS Halls in London each autumn. Incidentally, a visit to that annual event is very worth while, for it reveals not only to what extent these keenly competitive classes create a national interest, but also how beautiful and attractive things grown for food can look. It is an inspiration.

Undoubtedly, the best way to gain experience is to enter local shows. The usual number of vegetables needed is six, although there can be fewer, or more, according to the relevant rules and schedule, which have to be studied in order to conform.

I have proved many times that it is possible to grow the very best produce yet not gain the coveted awards, simply because one has not staged the exhibits advantageously. If only the competitor would take as much trouble over this as in the growing, many disappointments would be turned into triumphs.

Judges are only human, and have a lot of work to get through in the hour or two available between the staging of the exhibits and the opening of the show. They can be impressed at the outset by your use of every strategem to present your produce so that all the qualities are revealed and the weaknesses smothered. This is particularly so in the classes for collections.

Trays

Invariably, the schedule stipulates that the collection be on a tray not exceeding stated limits. It is best to have a special tray of boarding, or three-ply, to the exact size so that you have the fullest possible space for display. But instead of having it with a low floor surrounded by a ledge a few inches deep, you should make it so that its floor is well above table level. This makes your exhibit stand up proudly instead of appearing flat.

Next, if you are showing tall vegetables, such as leeks or celery, these must be stood upright; to support them there must be a light but firm framework at the extreme back, strictly vertical, to keep within the measurements (in case some pedantic judge wishes to disqualify anyone when he has the chance!) It must be securely fixed to the tray at the back, preferably with brackets such as can be obtained from the local ironmonger.

If you are showing onions, these should be placed on a box of peat or sand to keep them in position so that they all *look* the same size in depth, it being difficult to produce a number of onions all of the same dimensions.

Having placed the onion box, containing peat or sand, on the tray, you then put a cover over the lot including the back rack, using a piece of black cloth with matt side uppermost (Fig. 3). Do not fix it tightly, but have enough overlap for tucking underneath after you have put the finishing touches to your exhibit. Once you have obtained these pieces of equipment they will last for many years.

The exhibits

Firstly you fix the celery in position at one side of the back

25

Cross section

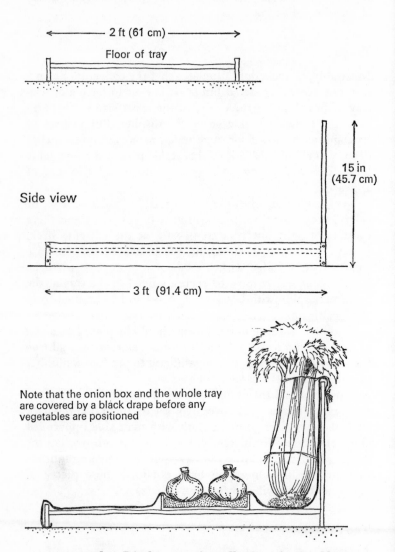

2 ft (61 cm)

Floor of tray

15 in
(45.7 cm)

Side view

3 ft (91.4 cm)

Note that the onion box and the whole tray
are covered by a black drape before any
vegetables are positioned

1, 2 and 3. Display tray for collection of vegetables

frame and then, on the other side, the leeks, after preparing them in the ways described under the relevant heading in later chapters. These vegetables are held by pieces of tape placed around their necks just below the leaves and fixed to the back frame by press pins pushed through the tape and the cloth into the woodwork. Or, if the backboard is not that high, it may be possible to loop the tape over the top edge and fasten it at the back.

If, instead of leeks and celery, you prefer to put cauliflowers at the back, the procedure is different. In this case you make a triangle of wood, put a black cloth over it, then drive in three nails from the back, the points (forming a triangle) coming through the cloth so that they project about 3 in (7·5 cm). On these you impale the cut stalks of the cauliflowers, these having the inner leaves intact but the outer ones trimmed off. You should measure distances so that the three cauliflowers practically touch each other and form a perfect triangle on the covered top part of the board. You then insert sprigs of curly parsley into the spaces around them using, if necessary, some greentwist into which you can tuck the stalks, so that there is a framework of three snow-white curds. The inner leaves are later trimmed back to the edges of the curds to reveal them in their complete purity.

It is best to have the cauliflower board the full width of

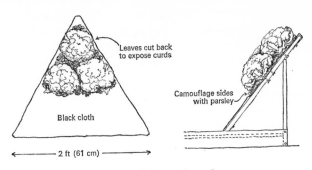

Leaves cut back
to expose curds

Camouflage sides
with parsley

Black cloth

2 ft (61 cm)

4. *Cauliflower board*

the tray so that these are held well above the onions which will be placed immediately in front. On the other hand, if you wish to show either celery or leeks, but not both, you can turn your cauliflower board around so that the three specimens are at one side, away from the onions and the other tall vegetable at the back.

Having placed your three back vegetables, with the onions towards the middle front, you then position the runner beans, or any other longish vegetable, while in the rest of the space you pile carrots, peas or potatoes, so making up the stipulated number.

The commonest mistake is to arrange these so that all their faults rather than their qualities are prominent. For example, some exhibitors will lay three carrots flat on one side of the tray and three on the other, painfully revealing all their defects, one being lack of uniformity. Instead, carefully select the best carrot of all, and then the next best two, and place on one side. Select the next best three specimens and place side by side on the tray; now take the two second best carrots and place them on the three, putting the best carrot of all on the top to form a ridge. This makes the utmost impression. To stop them tumbling, I have small pieces of lead placed on the tray, under the over-cloth; these can be adjusted without being visible to either the judges or the public, who often wonder how the vegetables are kept from sprawling.

In the case of potatoes, if the number needed is six, make a circle of five and then place the best one on the top to form a low mound with a focal point, rather than laying them out in a straight row which is often the method employed. When they are arrayed that way the judges are invited, as it were, to be critical, but when grouped or piled, they are disinclined to upset the arrangement, being content to look at the top ones and merely glancing at those underneath, in case there is any cheating.

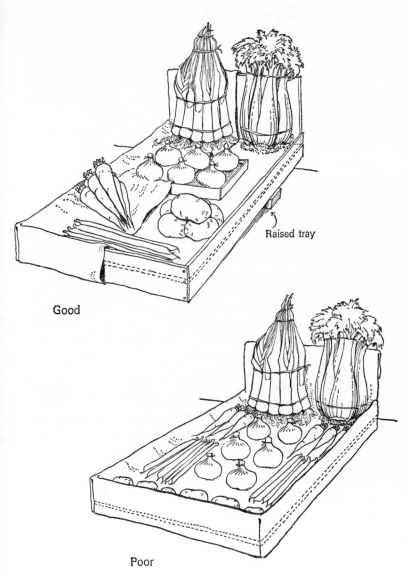

Raised tray

Good

Poor

5 and 6. Displaying a vegetable collection

Salads

Quite often there are classes for collections of salads. Whenever they are included I am inclined to enter them, especially if there are special prizes. Most times the sorts of things you can enter are stipulated, generally giving you a choice. For example, you may be invited to stage four salads from the following – 3 beet, 2 cucumber, 2 lettuce, 12 spring onions, 6 radishes or 6 tomatoes. The size of tray is generally limited to 18 in (45 cm) by 12 in (30 cm). If you have good lettuces always include them, as they form the essential ingredient of a salad. Indoor cucumbers and tomatoes are good, but the outdoor crops are not so favourable. Spring onions should be young with smallish bulbs and stems the size of pencils, the foliage being kept on and tied neatly with raffia. Wash the rootlets and leave them on. In fact, keep the onions intact except for removing an outer skin that will pull away very easily. Radishes should be young and fresh, their foliage retained, and tied into a neat bunch. The beet need much the same treatment; they should never be too large.

I find that, instead of black cloth as for vegetable trays, white tissue paper makes the best foundation for salads, and this is obtainable from any good friendly florist. It can, if the tray is merely a wooden framework, be fixed underneath with drawing pins.

Usually, parsley is allowed purely as dressing but other than using it to hide the outsides of cauliflowers, it is best not to worry about it. I think that it detracts from the actual exhibits and I have been with other judges who have been annoyed by its presence.

3

Potatoes

Potatoes are not very difficult to grow just for eating, but to get them to top exhibition standard is a different matter. It is not size that counts, but the emphasis is on quality; moderate proportions, and skins that are free from blemishes of any kind, while eyes must be very shallow. These qualities are obtained by choosing the right varieties, and treating the soil in the proper way for their development.

No matter what its type – clay, gravel, chalky, etc. – the chief thing is to work into it lots of humus-forming organic materials. One good way to do that is to dig deeply in autumn. As you do this, fork in as much manure or garden compost as you can. Then cover with the top spit without mixing anything at this stage. If you can, ridge it so that there are shallow furrows alternating at distances of 2 ft (60 cm). This will be right for the rows when planting time comes.

In late March, or early April, you re-shape the furrows, throwing the soil on to the ridges and then filling the furrows with anything that will give humus and the right texture for good root development. Among the materials you can use are garden compost, well-rotted manure, lawn mowings, oak and beech leafmould, sedge peat, fish meal, castor meal and decayed straw. A mixture is better than having one sort of material by itself. Spread along the furrow generously, and at the same time sprinkle a large handful of crushed wood charcoal to every yard length. Charcoal makes the potato skins bright.

Manures to avoid are spent mushroom compost or anything containing much lime, or lime by itself. These are apt to cause scabbiness.

If your ground is heavy and slug-infested, you can also sprinkle in some slug pellets; and if you think there are wireworms, you can include a little whizzed naphthalene. This is sometimes used to drive away millipedes, cutworms, carrot fly and onion fly.

Some exhibition growers dig a trench as for celery, line it with perforated polythene and then fill with a mixture of well-decayed manure and sedge peat, the soil itself doing no more than keeping the tubers cool and dark. The problem of earthing-up is overcome by a top-dressing in due course.

You plant your potatoes by nestling them in the organic material, spacing them 15 in (37·5 cm) apart. Cover over by levelling down the ridges. When planted at the right depth they are then covered with about 5 in (12 cm) of soil.

When the new growths peep through the ground it is best to draw soil over them whenever spring frosts threaten. They can also be protected by other means, such as putting sticks or hessian or plastic over them. The latter should be well suspended, or the damage may be worse than if they are frosted in the open. Eventually, earth-up in the usual way so that the furrows have now become the ridges.

Most gardeners sprout their sets (tubers) by packing them together in wooden trays, side by side with the rose ends upwards. If a little sedge peat is placed in the bottom it keeps them in position better. Stand the trays in a dark room, or in a shaded place in a cool greenhouse, but on no account must they be frosted. When the sprouting begins give them light so that they grow green and stubby. Some tubers produce many sprouts and when this happens you can rub off the weakest, so increasing the sizes of the resulting potatoes but reducing their numbers. But, as we do not want very large tubers for showing, this thinning of shoots should not be overdone. When sprouting, potatoes are prone to aphis (greenfly) attacks. Spray with one of the many pesticides available.

The best-sized sets resemble hen's eggs. Smaller sets can be planted more closely together, but they do not yield the best potatoes for showing. Larger sets should not be cut through. I know that this is frequently done, but the yields do not justify the treatment.

Varieties

Of the various types, those that have deep eyes are useless. Among the shallow-eyed, either round or kidney as the case may be, are Arran Comrade, Arran Supreme, Catriona, Di Vernon, Dr McIntosh, Homeguard, King Edward VII, Majestic, Pentland Dell, Pentland Lustre and Red King. Some are coloured. If the schedule stipulates what they are to be, care should be taken to ensure that you cannot be disqualified. Most times the ones with tinted eyes, such as Catriona or King Edward VII, are accepted as coloured varieties.

Due to modern financial difficulties many old show potatoes are going out of commercial cultivation, therefore it is impossible to buy Scotch or Irish seed of those varieties. Once you have a favourite which is not popular, nor familiar, you should take care to preserve it year after year, rather than heed the traditional advice always to get fresh seed. There are ways of doing it successfully. One method is, instead of planting all your show potatoes in April, to hold some back, keeping them in a shaded cool shed until the end of July. Then plant them in a row elsewhere in the garden. The outcome will be smallish tubers just right for sets by the beginning of October, when the foliage is still green. They must be lifted and stored in a cool frostproof place. Usually these

B

will be just as good, or even better, than any commercially available sets. It is possible to have your own strain of prize-winning potatoes, keeping them year after year in this way. I have a friendly rival who is very successful with this method.

In dry seasons potatoes should be given lots of water. They suffer more from drought than other vegetables.

The crop is best left in the gound until the day before exhibiting. However, if the weather is inclement it may pay to be two days ahead, but potatoes quickly take on a green tinge when exposed, and although showmen sometimes manage to keep the same tubers for two or three successive shows, the majority of judges quickly spot this and decide against them.

When lifted, the potatoes should come out cleanly. The ones to select will be of medium size and shapely, according to their variety. In local shows the kidneys most favoured are about 4 in (10 cm) long. At national shows a slightly larger size is usually preferred. After digging, I like to pick up a potato of about the desired size and then look for others as near as possible to match it. If they cannot be found, then a slightly smaller size is selected and there are generally more of these to choose from. Those selected should exceed the number wanted, for the chances are that some will reveal blemishes after the skins have been cleaned.

If possible use tepid soft water for cleaning. Have two pails; into one squirt just a little washing-up liquid. Immerse the potato and gently apply a soft sponge to the skin and eyes. That done, immediately gently swill it in the other bucket, which should contain pure soft water, holding it in your hand to wash off the detergent. Place each potato on an old towel or piece of sacking, and when all have been cleaned and rinsed cover with another old cloth. They dry quickly and can then be sorted over and packed in old rags or anything suitable you can find, in readiness for the journey to the show venue.

Staging

In most village shows the six potatoes for exhibit are usually laid flat on the tabling, two by two, or three by three, side by side. They look much better if arranged on a shallow plain plate so that one potato, the best you can find, is laid on the top of the other four or five. This gives your exhibit 'lift' and makes a good first impression. I always believe in first impressions.

4
Onions

Whenever onions are mentioned among gardeners, there are always some who deplore the large specimens seen in national or local shows, while others will wonder how ever the growers managed to get them to such sizes. Unless there is a champion in the district, the ordinary gardener can grow them larger than his competitors by adopting a method of culture that is different to what they envisage. It is thought that size is attained by feeding the plants with special fertilisers when they are in the development stage. But to do that not only spoils the onions, it also impairs their keeping qualities. Regarding quality, if grown as I now suggest, the resultant crop will be superior to many outdoor-sown bulbs, and will keep quite sound until the early spring if hung in an open shed. The only drawback with large onions grown in this way is that one specimen is a lot to use immediately, in spite of its being juicy, tender and of mild flavour. I have cultivated them over many years to sizes that easily gain awards at local shows, although they do not attain the standards of the champions.

Contrary to the advice proffered for vegetables in general, it is good to grow onions on the same site year after year provided disease does not make this impracticable. By digging deeper each autumn, and adding the right sort of richness every season, there is a build-up of the perfect condition for this crop.

In the first instance you bastard-trench the site. This means digging the top spit, keeping it above all the time, and then digging up the lower spit, and keeping it below. Into the bottom spit you mix all the garden compost, old pea haulms, or spent mushroom compost that you possibly can, while into the top spit you mix more rotted manure, peat, or anything that is decayed, which will soon be converted to humus. It can be mixed-in to within an inch or two of the surface.

I have myself sometimes not dug the ground so deeply, but worked in all the strong manure I can, simply by turning it in the depth of the spade. That done, I have put another layer of manure on the surface, and then covered that with soil taken off the garden at each side to form a raised bed, as is made for asparagus.

If done in autumn, the bed can be top-dressed a few weeks later with basic slag at the rate of about a half pound (224 g) per square yard (1 sq m). (This fertiliser is becoming increasingly difficult to get. Instead, I have used horticultural gypsum, a form of lime that has a beneficial effect upon manures.) Nothing more is done to the bed until late April, when it is time to put the seedlings in their parmenent positions.

Seed Sowing

It is necessary to choose varieties that will make large bulbs. There are small firms who have their own special strains and varieties but some of the largest are somewhat coarse and undesirable. For most gardens, when all things are considered – quality, size, keeping propensities, and uni-formity – Selected Ailsa Craig is quite satisfactory. You will seldom grow four-pounders of this variety, but you can get them to half that weight in perfect form.

The seed is sown in pans or boxes of John Innes Seed Compost just after Christmas in a cool greenhouse with a minimum temperature of 12°C (55°F). Covered by glass and shaded in the usual way it soon germinates, when all the light possible should be given the seedlings. When they are at the stage of uncurling their leaves they are transplanted into other boxes of John Innes Seed Compost, spacing them about 2 in (5 cm) apart in all directions. I generally like to put the strongest ones separately into 3-in (7·5 cm) pots that are deeper than usual. The seedlings are kept growing in the greenhouse until the end of March, when they are moved to a cold frame and gradually inured to the elements, in readiness for planting in the bed in late April.

Near the time of planting the bed is dressed with a 'complete' fertiliser, such as Growmore, at the rate of about 3 oz (85 g) per square yard (1 sq m), and raked down into a friable state. It is only lightly firmed just so that the soil does not crumble when holes are made with a trowel. Spacings for the plants are a foot apart in rows 15 in (37·5 cm) asunder. With the line taut, the trowel is pushed down to form a wall, against which is put the plant, with its long roots placed straight down; the soil is then pushed towards it and made moderately firm. The right depth is for the base of the main stem to be an inch (2·5 cm) below the surface when all is levelled. There is nothing more to do except to keep weeds at bay and look out for any diseases or pests that may appear.

As a safeguard, rather than a cure, I like to water with Cheshunt Compound when the seedlings are in the pans or pots and again just after they have been 'pricked out' to guard against 'damping off'. In the garden, onion fly may attack, but I've been lucky. I invariably grow a row of parsley against the bed to ward it off. However, as a further preventative, if 4 per cent calomel dust is used, putting a little of it around each seedling after planting, it not only dissuades the fly but also checks white rot. It needs about a pound for every 50-ft (15-m) run. Repeat three weeks after the first dose. Later still I give a dressing of Benlate according to instruction, to guard against rot and also mildew.

There are other pests, such as eelworm and thrips, that may make it necessary to change the site. The chemists are constantly finding new ways to combat troubles and we should heed them. However, over the years, I have found that those bothers are no more likely to occur than are the dangerous diseases that afflict human beings. If they occur they must be dealt with by the latest antidotes. Most times it is best not to worry.

If the seedlings grow nicely in the outdoor bed they can be given a tonic of nitrogen (saltpetre) in a mild way in June during showery weather. However, on no account should they be dressed during dry weather and it is unwise to apply anything after midsummer.

Towards the end of July, the bulbs will be swelling nicely. At this stage you carefully inspect each one, scraping away a little of the surface soil at the base; at the same time, pull away the rough outer skin, leaving a clean appearance. The sun will turn the pale outside to a beautiful golden hue. It is too late to perform this exercise less than a fortnight before a show, and it is disastrous to peel the bulbs once they are lifted. If the weather is inclement, a polythene umbrella-like covering can be supplied to stop the bulbs from spoiling or continuing to develop 'bull' necks.

Ripening the bulbs is an important part of preparation. As well as peeling off the extreme loose outer skin a fortnight or so before a show, it is, if the plants are still growing, advisable to bend over the tops to check growth and at the same time insert a fork deeply under each bulb and gently loosen it, so breaking the long deep roots below, but not lifting sufficiently for the bulbs to rock or become unseated.

They need to be lifted two or three days before the event and laid in an outdoor sunny position or open shed if it rains. Do not put them where they can be scorched, as in a greenhouse. Trim off the rootlets close to the base, and only remove any very loose outer skin. Never peel. Cut off the tops to within 2 in (5 cm) of the bulbs, then fold these over and tie tightly with raffia. This is the normal procedure if the tops are strong, but if they have shrunk through ripening they look better if tied at the thinnest part of the neck, and then cut immediately above.

If the onions are to be shown in a collection of vegetables, I like to place an ordinary bedding-plant box filled with soft sand under the black cloth (see page 26) and then make a nest for each specimen, pressing the sand around according to its size, so that when the half dozen have been put in position they appear to be precisely alike along the top. When they are shewn in single-dish classes, they are usually simply sat on cardboard rings, as are eggs placed in their cups.

Sets

There is often some confusion in the onion classes through bad wording of the schedule. Some will argue that onions raised in the greenhouse as described are not 'spring-sown', but unless stated that the entries should be 'grown in the open' or something like that, the majority of judges agree that these monsters are 'according to schedule'.

Where a schedule does not stipulate the type of onion, those grown from sets instead of seed are admissible, but they rarely come up to the standard of the seed-sown specimens. Sometimes there are classes for bulbs grown from sets. The soil is prepared well beforehand and the sets planted quite early, depending on the weather. Whenever I grow a crop for this class, just to obtain additional points for a cup in this section, I plant them singly in pots of John Innes Seed Compost during February and keep them in the greenhouse until the middle of April. This gives them a good start, but they will never attain the proportions of a good seed strain.

Because of the increasing skill of champion onion growers, combined with the special varieties they can obtain, some show committees are restricting the sizes allowed, much as they do for pompom dahlias. There is either a weight limit or a diameter control. In this case the chief advantage is to get a variety that matures early and produces a beautiful bronzy-yellow skin. There are F.1 hybrids most useful for this, such as Buccaneer or Superba. With these I like to sow seed in boxes in the greenhouse in the latter half of February, and then plant out in a bed that has been more leniently treated than for the giants.

Spring Onions

Where there are salad classes, spring onions should be included if you have them. The variety to grow is White Lisbon. You sow outdoors in late spring for autumn shows, and simply pull them just before the event, trimming off the rootlets, pulling off the loose outer skin and tying into a bunch, leaving the tops intact.

Shallots

Most flower shows have classes for shallots, and most of them are very popular. This is because these vegetables are not difficult to grow. Quite often there are two classes, i.e. one for small specimens suitable for pickling, and one for those described as 'giant'. You will find them displayed in all manner of ways, such as on saucers of sawdust, if the tiny ones, or in special boxes if giants. It doesn't matter as long as the container is of the right size and keeps the bulbs in formation. The awards often depend upon the whims of the judges. I have seen an exhibit staged in a village show gain the top award, but when the identical bulbs were put in a neighbouring event, they were simply ignored, although the rest of the entries were much the same in both shows.

However, heed the schedule. If it states 'large', get your largest. If it states 'picklers', choose those that are under an inch across at the waist. Have them as even as possible, and get them well-ripened by harvesting a few weeks before the show and placing them in the sunshine by day, taking them in at night. They should have thin necks, and each can be tied at the top with a piece of raffia, or they can be twisted without tying.

There are two main sorts of shallot, the Dutch Yellow (of a golden brown or straw colour) and the large Russian Red. You can raise the latter from seed. The Dutch Yellow is the most likely variety to please the judges.

5
Root Vegetables

CARROTS

From the exhibitor's point of view, after potatoes and onions, carrots are the next important vegetable. There are generally a number of classes in the summer schedules, while for collections they are safer point-getters than some of the other quality vegetables. For those reasons I grow a limited quantity of them by a special method that will usually produce just the right sort of specimens that will appeal to visitors and judges alike.

The worst enemy of the carrot is the fly that spoils the roots, while the chief fault is, if grown in ordinary garden soil such as mine, they inevitably become coarse and crooked. My method of growing overcomes both problems.

I take wooden boxes and remove their lids and bases, and place them on a deeply dug part of the garden and fill with sandy compost. These boxes need to be at least 18 in (45 cm) deep for short carrots but 6 in (15 cm) deeper for long varieties. Some old gardeners use barrels, such as the Australian apples arrive in. If I cannot get boxes I knock posts into the ground and board up round them, so making bins of the right depth, about a foot wide, and any length to fit the garden.

The soil I use happens to be a natural mixture of leafmould

and greensand but, failing that, the compost of past crops, such as used for chrysanthemums or tomatoes, is fine. After knocking out the roots, the compost is shaken through a $\frac{1}{4}$-in (6 mm) mesh sieve, and a little Growmore fertiliser mixed into it, before being put in the bins or boxes. This is generally prepared around Christmas time, to allow settling down naturally before sowing time in April. As a precaution, wire netting is placed over the top to keep cats from using them.

If the weather is dry, a good watering is given a few days before intending to sow, using the perforated hose, so that there is a thorough slow soaking. If weeds germinate, so much the better for they can be pulled out. When the top becomes cleanly workable, the seed is sown. Shallow drills are made with a label or pencil, spacing these about 6 in (15 cm) across, in whichever direction is best. The seed is sown thinly in the drills, and then covered over by smoothing the surface with the hand. A light watering with a fine-rosed can is given before sheets of glass are laid over the top, these being supported by the sides of the boxes, and over the glass is placed some dark polythene or some similar material to shut out light.

Carrot seed suffers if the soil is too dry and will sometimes perish because of lack of moisture. This is avoided by putting the seed in a gauze bag and placing this in a bowl or jar of tepid water for twenty-four hours immediately prior to sowing. This treatment together with the protection of glass and covering will most times give a quick start, and a good growth is assured. The cover and the glass should be removed immediately there is evidence of growth or the seedlings will quickly spoil through being drawn.

At first, they may need watering in dry weather, but once they are growing it will not be necessary to apply the per-forated hose unless the weather is unusually dry. The roots will grow down into the base of the boxes and, if necessary, into the garden soil. They should be thinned while young, leaving those that look best for showing, until they are 6 in (15 cm) apart in all directions. The thinnings are delicious.

There are usually classes for both short and long carrots. By 'short' is meant stump-rooted, and by 'long' is meant those with tapering roots. Quite often I've seen 'long' carrots shorter than the 'short' ones, and the judges have considered both favourably. However, it is best to grow varieties noted for their qualities in both shape and appearance. One of the best stump-rooted is Chantenay Red Cored (Suttons' Favourite), while for a long-rooted class I prefer to grow New Red Intermediate, rather than St Valery which is often favoured by other competitors.

To combat the carrot fly, you merely brush the outsides of the boxes or bins with creosote during early May. Done earlier, the smell may evaporate before the fly is active. As this pest usually keeps close to the ground it is unlikely to attack crops grown in this way. And once the plants are developing nicely, if you mulch between them with thin applications of lawn mowings, not only does this deter the fly, it also keeps the crowns of the roots quite fresh and of the right colour, which is not the case with roots grown in the ordinary way.

When lifting time comes, a day before the show, the stump-rooted ones will come up easily, but the tapered varieties have to be got out of their compost very carefully, for broken tips are regarded as faults. Wash them gently with a soft cloth or sponge, in water to which has been added just a squirt of washing-up liquid. Rinse them in fresh water immediately. Snip off any hairs carefully with a pair of scissors. Wrap up each root in a damp flannel or cloth and keep moist until showing time. If carrots are taken from moist ground and then placed in dry air they will suddenly split, and the whole operation be in vain. Cut off the tops leaving about an inch of stalk, and tie these together with a piece of raffia.

The usual way to stage in special classes is to place the

carrots flat on the tabling, but they can be made to look much more important if arranged on a suitable platter. This should be rather flat, and broad enough to hold three of the carrots side by side, putting the poorest specimen of the half dozen in the middle. They can be kept from rolling by plugging each side of the outer-placed carrots with a roll of paper held in position by the dip in the plate. On the first three place the next two best specimens, the final one at the top being the best of the lot.

PARSNIPS

Parsnips are not good vegetables for showing during August, but they are held in high esteem for those October exhibitions where classes are included as incidental to the flowers and fruits. In collections they are not top-pointers, although a number of judges are inclined to require them to be super to justify high marks. They can be useful, when there is no special class for them, for entry in the class 'any other vegetable'. They will most times be regarded more favourably than such things as salsify or celeriac.

The usual way for growing for showing is to make deep holes, quite 2 ft (60 cm) down, with a crowbar, and twist and bend it round and round to form a deep elongated funnel. Into this is put similar compost to that described for carrots. Three seeds are sown on each funnel or cone, during March, and eventually reduced to one seedling when they are large enough for the best to be chosen.

The great problem is to lift the roots intact at showing time, and should they be crooked or defective a number are spoiled before the right ones are found. It is very hard work and hardly worth the bother. You can grow them in the same way as carrots, i.e. in raised boxes or beds. But being heftier the containers have to be fairly hefty too. There are some gardeners who grow them in large clay chimney pots, inserting these halfway into the soil. However, I confess that I seldom bother with this vegetable myself.

A good long-rooted variety is named Exhibition, while another is Tender and True. There are stump-rooted and intermediate varieties, such as White Gem, that are not half the trouble to grow and are useful at times.

Parsnips are subject to attack from the carrot fly and also the celery fly. Canker is a troublesome disease making the skin go rusty; over-rich soil and a wet autumn cause this problem. Growing by the raised-bed method in poorish soil is one way to combat it. For show preparation, use the same method as for carrots.

BEET

Showing beet is somewhat of a gamble. There is usually a considerable number of entries because they are so easy to grow. The judging method is to have either the root end of the beef cut off or a wedge taken out, and the colour compared with all the rest. I have many times gained the prize when I least expected it, through sheer luck. However, when lifting I take the greatest care not to damage the roots in any way, and to wash the beet without injuring the skin. The leaves are left intact and just tied to form a neat bunch. The R.H.S Horticultural Show Handbook says that these leaves should be cut off, as for carrots, etc. I've never known anyone to be disqualified for not doing so. I think that any injury of any kind affects the colour of the flesh.

The roots should be of good appearance and of a nice size. They should not be quite as large as a tennis ball nor as small as a golf ball. Sow the seed in May for August showing. As long as the soil in which they are grown does not contain fresh manure, it matters very little. A dressing of agricultural salt when the roots are forming is helpful.

There are two distinct types, the round and the long. Long beet have the best colour but are seldom seen in village flower shows except in the north of Britain. Seed is rarely included in modern catalogues. Should you be able to obtain it, and have a nice sandy garden, it may be an interesting experiment to grow and show the deep-blood-red sort. However, if round beet is specified, as is usual, the variety most likely to win is named Globe. Another is Boltardy. When you lift them, a day or so before the show, look carefully at the base around the taproot. It should be a nice dark colour. If it isn't, your chances of winning are remote!

TURNIPS

The growing and preparation of these is very similar to that for beet, but instead of leaving the foliage on the roots, it is cut off about 3 in (7·5 cm) from the neck and the stalks are then tied together with raffia. Evenness and cleanness of skin are paramount. They should never be pithy, for invariably the judges cut through one to test for quality.

There are various types, some elongated, some with orange skins, some with purple and white skins and some that are pure white. The most attractive are the latter, the variety Snowball being the most shapely. Desirable specimens should be slightly larger than a tennis ball. Sow in May for August showing. The chief problem in dry weather is combating fly. In dry seasons this vegetable is best not bothered about for August shows.

SALSIFY AND SCORZONERA

Sometimes the roots of these are shown in a class for unusual vegetables, but from the showman's point of view they are not worth growing unless the householder has a taste for them, and then they can sometimes be exhibited as incidental novelties.

6

Peas and Beans

PEAS

Peas are among the top-point vegetables and it needs considerable skill to get them to exhibition standards for August shows. Most times there are very few entries, so if you can manage to grow them well it is a worthy achievement likely to be most successful, both in the individual classes and in collections.

A sunny position, and ground well dug and manured as for onions and potatoes is most suitable. I like to prepare the site in autumn and then dress the surface with hydrated lime in spring. As peas produce their own nitrogen, any fertiliser containing much of this element is not good.

Instead of sowing in the normal way, you draw one straight drill and space the peas 3 in (7·5 cm) apart singly. When they come through, give the requisite supports, preferably trimmed peasticks to which they can cling, and if any plants develop strong branching growths pinch them back. Should all the peas germinate it is as well to reduce the plants by half, so spacing them 6 in (15 cm) apart.

I am reluctant to give peas much water during dry hot summers, for it is inclined to make the foliage go yellow and deterioration quickly sets in. However, while young they can be given a gentle soaking and then be mulched alongside the rows, so conserving moisture and making artificial watering unnecessary.

One important factor is timing. You can calculate that you should sow about eleven weeks before the vegetable is needed. Supposing the show is to be on 15th August, a short row should be sown during the last few days of May, and another during the middle of the first week of June. Another important calculation is that it takes about three weeks from the time the flowers open before the pods become filled with peas at the right state of perfection, which means they must be fresh and yet developed. Therefore, should the flowers arrive too early they should be picked off to induce others to follow them.

The best varieties are the trusted and tried ones known by every gardener, rather than novelties of any sort. Among these are Suttons' Show Perfection, Onward, Achievement and Alderman. These all need staking and the height should be heeded, taking into consideration that they will grow rather taller on the single-stem system. Never rely upon one long row of a single variety. Only a few plants are necessary to get the desired number of pods. Better to have short rows of a selection, for each behaves differently in accordance with the season.

Three things to guard against are mildew, thrips and maggots. Mildew generally comes when the ground becomes dry. Mulching does much to waylay this. Both for thrip and the pea moth which causes the maggots, the best antidote is dimethoate of which there are several brands. It is an organophosphorous systemic and attention should be given to the instructions for its use. An alternative is to dust the plants while in flower with Sevin Dust. This is effective against the maggot but may not be so for thrip.

When peas are gathered for show, great care should be taken not to rub the pods, so removing the 'bloom' and spoiling the appearance. Take each one by the stem and clip it off the haulm with a pair of scissors, and then place on the flat surface of a container lined with something soft like cotton wool. If you hold each pod up to the sky you can usually see the peas inside, you can then carefully select those that are evenly filled. Although they are normally laid flat on the staging without trimmings and sometimes made to form a 'Catherine Wheel', they are better placed on a suitably sized plate covered with clean tissue paper. Place them in two layers and then put the best pod of all across the top. This is most probably the one the judges will open; they will usually fall for this 'bait'.

RUNNER BEANS

Although it is generally recommended, quite rightly, that for the successful growing of runner beans the soil should have been deeply trenched and well manured the previous autumn, I have obtained my best beans from a garden that has an awful clay subsoil a foot below the surface. I have an idea that it contains some sort of mineral beneficial to the bean. The lower clay has only been loosened, while plenty of manure has been worked into the top and a dressing of gypsum lime given.

But success lies not only in the preparation of the ground; it is necessary to start the seed by sowing separately in largish pots, in good soil such as John Innes, the best time being the second half of April. The resulting seedlings should not be planted out before the beginning of June, especially if the nights are frosty, for they are very tender.

The aim is to get long even pods of good colour, free from blemishes of any kind. They should be straight and contain no prominent seeds. The judges invariably break one or two to test for fleshiness, lack of beans, and freedom from stringiness. When grown well, I regard them as being preferable to some of the higher-pointing vegetables in collections, especially if any of the top class are doubtful. The individual classes are most keenly contested, for everyone seems to be able to grow them, although not to perfection.

New varieties keep coming along, each proclaimed to be the longest and the best for both culinary and exhibition purposes. At the time of writing the one most favoured is Enorma. Only last year I gained a first prize for 'longest runner bean' taken from this variety grown on clay.

A support of special bean sticks is essential, either erected in a long strong double row, or, which I prefer, a wigwam-style series of clumps. First, let the chief growth of each plant entwine itself to the top and then start pinching out long sideshoots, so concentrating the flowering. Ultimately, the pods will form in the bunch. To get show beans you reduce the numbers on each to either one or two, so that all nourishment goes into those remaining. You can calculate that those small pods that appear about fifteen days before the date of the show will be the right size when you require them.

Quite often, runner beans fail to pod-set, the flowers dropping off instead. Contrary to usual beliefs, it is of little use to spray them with clear water. Pollination must be carried out by insects, or you can attempt to do it yourself with a brush by squeezing the middle of the flower until you can insert a camel hair. This is done from the left side of the front of the flower. While syringing with clear water is wrong when flowers are dropping, at the beginning of the season some growers mix up a weak sugar solution and spray the plants lightly. This attracts all the bees in the near neighbourhood, and many of them will then deal with the flowers.

There are some growers who advise nitrogenous fertilisers. I do not think that fertilisers ever do runner beans any good. Gypsum, wood ashes, or bonemeal worked into the ground long before the beans are planted will help, but after that stage it is best to forget chemicals.

Gather the pods a day before the show by snipping them

off with scissors and placing them carefully into a flat lined box or basket. Some will curve and few will be straight. To get them to look like the best in the show is not difficult. You take an old towel, or linen teacloth (actually I use a cut-open length of discarded pyjama leg), soak it in water, squeeze out firmly and then lay it flat on the potting-shed bench. Next, take a straight piece of hazel wood, or something similar, about 18 in (45 cm) long and place across the end of the cloth, and curl it over. Now take the first bean and place it alongside, and curl that over. Add the other beans, one by one, until all are in a thick roll. As you place them in position, bend each as straight as you dare without snapping the bean in two. Left like that until the morning of the show it is surprising how most of them will have conformed to the same pattern of straightness and freshness. Carry them to the show still rolled in the cloth, always having a few spares in case some are too old, or beany, or thin. Judges snap one or two through to see whether they lack stringiness, and developed seeds are much frowned upon. At most shows you have to lay the beans out side by side. If there are variations, mix them about well, rather than grading them so that longest are to one side and shortest the other. Let the judges make the comparisons.

DWARF OR FRENCH BEANS

Dwarf beans do not require as much growing as runners. The plants should be thinned out to a foot apart, but never the crop itself. Sow outdoors in May for August shows. Do not fall for novel sorts, but rely upon standard varieties such as The Prince and Masterpiece. The Prince gives us long very narrow round fleshy pods so fancied by the judges. The first thing they do is compare for length, freshness and evenness and then snap one or maybe two in half to check for stringiness. There should be no seeds that can swell the exterior

53

of the pods. Gather the beans the day before the show and wrap in a moist cloth, as recommended for runner beans. If they are to be included in a collection, it should be one of a dozen sorts or more. There are generally separate classes for them.

BROAD BEANS

These are not often allotted classes, and as they are low-pointers in collections, and August is getting rather late in their season, it is hardly worth the bother to grow them for exhibition. However, if there is a class for a small collection of vegetables at a June event, (rose or sweet pea show), it may then be very useful. There are Longpod and Windsor varieties. The Longpods win the prizes when they are in good condition. The pods should be filled, but never be old. The worst thing that can happen is when a judge opens a pod to find that the bean has become dark at the eye. Skins should look nicely green and fresh, and staged as pulled straight off the plants without any form of preparation. If they are in excellent condition they can be placed across a plate in a neat pile, best on top, to enhance presentation, otherwise just lay them out side by side on the tabling.

7

Stem Vegetables

CELERY

When celery is grown well and is shown in vegetable collections it gets high marks from the adjudicators, although it is really too early for home consumption. As there are often classes for it in flower show schedules, a few plants can be grown specially for exhibition.

Instead of putting the seedlings in trenches in the ordinary way they are best planted on flat beds, after preparing the ground as described on p. 31 for potatoes. As the celery plantings should not be put out in the garden before late May, all that is done earlier is to level down the ridges that have been previously prepared. Celery is moisture-loving and grows well where there is a lot of dead vegetation; therefore, if manure, peat or other materials – as recommended for potatoes – are incorporated, so much the better.

The seed should be sown in pans and the seedlings later 'pricked out' into a deepish box as soon as they are large enough to handle. A warm greenhouse is necessary for the earliest crop, a temperature of 15°C (60°F) being required for germination, which is rather slow. First sowings can be made in the middle of February, but the easiest to rear are those raised from seed sown in early March. John Innes

Seed Compost makes a nice medium; however, if sedge peat is added to it, the mixture gives the plants a better start. An important factor is always to keep the seedlings equably warm while in the greenhouse where they are kept until late April; they are then moved to the cold frame, where they are protected from frosts and cold nights while being hardened-off before transfer to the open garden.

The box into which the small seedlings are transplanted should be at least 4 in (10 cm) deep, and they should be spaced 3 in (7·5 cm) apart, using John Innes Seed Compost, as for the original sowing, to which has been added peat, as for the seedpan. Keep the roots moist, for only a brief drying-out will cause a check and produce pithy stems. The whole secret of growing celery, whether for exhibition or for home consumption, is to always keep the roots evenly moist, whether in the seedpan, the boxes, or in the garden.

There are three types of celery: the traditional pink and white varieties whose names vary from catalogue to catalogue; the self-blanching type; and the green American – this last never needing blanching, being edible as it is. It never wins prizes, not does it find favour on the table. The self-blanching variety is good for cooking but not so acceptable for eating raw. I have staged the latter in vegetable classes quite success-fully, but only when my rivals have not included the good old-fashioned celery in their exhibits. The white varieties grow more quickly then the pink versions of the standard type, but the latter are deemed superior.

Planted in the garden on the flat bed with as little root disturbance as possible, using a trowel to scoop the holes and the fingers to push soil back around them, the young plants should be spaced about a foot apart in all directions. Kept weeded and watered, if the weather is dry, they are ready for the first stage of blanching when considerably over a foot high. Take pieces of ordinary brown wrapping paper, cut into squares of about 8 in × 8 in (20 cm × 20 cm) and wrap one of these around the lower part of each plant, after removing any loose or decaying leaves, tying it with raffia at top and bottom. Do not make it too tight, leaving some room for plant development. About a fortnight later, apply another square of paper slightly overlapping the top edge of the previous piece. After another fortnight, remove the two wrappings, examine the plants to see if all is well, and then replace the wrappings and also put above them a third wrapping; this should be ample, although experts may put a fourth one around if growth is abundant.

If the plants are growing nicely throughout this period, you can put some liquid fertiliser in a watering can and apply to the roots at fortnightly intervals. Some growers use nitrate of soda for this. However, always remember that celery likes a lot of moisture at the roots.

When you lift your plants for show, you merely pick off any decaying or discoloured foliage and select those that have blanched the most successfully. The sticks are held together by a ring of raffia just below the leaves. The rough parts of the roots are shaved away, but it is a mistake to cut the core hard back. Rather, you can wrap it around with a piece of dark polythene (to form a cup when tied to the neck between the stems and the root bunch) into which some water can be placed to keep the plant fresh – if you are staging it in a collection. If to be laid flat in a single class, you do not add water, but if tied this way *it looks good!*

CELERIAC

Celeriac, unlike celery, is not a high-pointing vegetable, therefore it should never be included in a collection. However, it may be useful in a class of its own, or where there is an invitation to show 'Any other vegetable not enumerated in any class'. It can also be put in a salad collection unless otherwise stipulated. To prepare for show, you merely wash the root, trim back the rough stringy bits, and the foliage, for it is the big core that is used. It should be grown similarly to celery, but blanching is unnecessary.

LEEKS

While I am not fond of leeks for August shows, there are often classes for them, and as they get the maximum in collections it is worth while growing just a small number for the purpose.

The seed should be sown in the greenhouse, in precisely the same way as for onions, although the end of January rather than late December is early enough. They should be pricked out into deepish boxes or singly into small pots and kept growing in the greenhouse until late April when they can be placed in the cold frame for hardening off, and eventually planted in the garden.

The best variety is the Lyon-Prizetaker. An alternative is Musselburgh.

The best site is one prepared as for celery on the flat; in fact, these two crops are best grown side by side in a prepared plot so that they can be kept watered and given fertilisers simultaneously.

Both need blanching, but instead of using brown paper as for celery, the usual method is to grow leeks in land drain-pipes (tiles), that are a foot long and 3 in (7·5 cm) in diameter. These are carefully placed over the plants when the latter are about 15 in (37·5 cm) high at the part where the foliage bends over. They are kept watered, and given a dilute solution of fertiliser about once a fortnight. They are seldom any bother in any other way. Some exhibitors nip off the tops when they become at all straggly, so causing the necks to increase in size.

When the time comes to 'lift' the leeks for the show, dig up each whole plant carefully, together with the pipe. Trim off the lower roots until it is possible to pull the pipe off from that end. The roots to choose should not have large bulbous swellings at the bottom, but taper up to the neck and be beautifully blanched. Do not remove more of the outer sheaths than is absolutely necessary, for this is frowned upon by judges. Trim off the rough bits of leaves at the top, and then lay the leeks on the bench to form a nice flat pile, selecting the best ones for the top. Tie with raffia around the lower stems and also around the necks to keep them together neatly. Then collect the foliage together at the top, tying neatly with raffia and nipping off any that spoil the appearance. Place flat on the tabling for the single classes. For collections, see Chapter One.

RHUBARB

Seeing that rhubarb is a stem vegetable, it is given a mention here. It should only be exhibited when there are classes for it, it being useless in collections of any kind. Where there are classes the chief qualities should be freshness, length, good colouring and evenness. Pull from the crown, trim off the leaves leaving just a little piece at the top; tie the requisite number of stems together at both ends with raffia and place on the show table. On one occasion, I was given first prize for a specified number of sticks. When I got them home I discovered I had put in one too many. Unluckily for my rivals, the judges hadn't noticed the error!

8

Greenstuff

To the average gardener, all members of the cabbage tribe are known as brassicas. But he may be surprised that swedes, radishes, turnips, kohl-rabi, rutabaga and other similar forms of edible vegetation also belong to that family. Where applicable they are considered in other chapters. Here, we deal only with the kinds that conform to the description of greenstuff.

CAULIFLOWERS (See Fig. 4)

Of the huge assortment, the most important are cauliflowers. They are the only brassicas eligible for top points in collections, but the chief difficulty is to have specimens in a perfect state during August when most flower shows are held. At one time, the white-headed broccoli were considered to be distinct from cauliflowers, but all are now classed as being one and the same – the only difference being the time of maturity. As far as I know none of the old broccoli 'turn-in' during August, but there are other vegetables that produce bunched heads, mostly the tinted varieties such as calabrese, that are now classed as broccoli, so making a distinction between the two names.

Cauliflowers can be grown to mature between June and November. The late ones are grown from seed sown outdoors in the ordinary way, and transplanted. Those we need for August showing are usually sown in early March indoors.

The variety that has stood the test for years is All The Year Round. New ones come along, such as The Beacon and Dominant, but seem not to be so reliable for turning-in at the right time. Seed quickly germinates in a cool greenhouse, and seedlings should be transplanted to deepish boxes or individually into temporary pots, and eventually be hardened-off in a frame.

They can be planted out towards the middle or end of April quite safely. The position should be a sunny one, the soil must be rich and firm and never allowed to become dry. Once cauliflower roots suffer from thirst, small curds will result instead of those the size of large inverted saucers. Some even 'go blind' and produce nothing at all.

The best cauliflowers I ever saw staged at an August show were grown throughout in a cool greenhouse, with no heat from Easter onwards. They were planted in a deepish border that had produced a crop of tomatoes in the previous season.

When the heads eventually 'turn-in', some of the inner leaves should be broken at the rib and bent over to keep the curd from going yellow through too much exposure to light. It is not much use showing cauliflowers, especially in collections, if they are defective in any way. Not only should they be milk-white, or whiter, the shape should be symmetrical, the sections close together and compact. Another drawback, apart from poor shape and colour, is a frothy appearance. When you cut them, leave a fair number of leaves intact, merely shortening the outer ones for convenience. Never remove them close to the curd. On the show day, cut back all the leaves neatly except the tiny ones just peeping over the edges of the curd, so that they look fresh up to the last minute. Always keep the curd covered for as long as possible.

CABBAGES

If you sow at the right times and select the most suitable varieties, you can cut cabbages throughout the year. The ones most suitable for showing during August should be sown outdoors in early April, and be transplanted directly they are large enough to handle into well-prepared ground that is rich and firm. As they grow, when the weather is damp or if the ground has been well watered, a little fertiliser such as Growmore can be applied occasionally. Great size is not desirable – you need sound solid heads of modest proportions. The judges invariably push their hands in between the heads and the outer leaves to see how firm the middles are.

At one time the most favoured variety was Winnigstadt. It is a compact cabbage with a pointed heart, very good looking, and generally matures in August. However, when well grown, some of the rounder 'Primo' type are preferred, especially the newish F.1 hybrids. These are so uniform in character and as uniformity is a quality, it has to be considered. Outer leaves are also taken into account. They should not be stripped off. Freedom from caterpillars and a general wholesome freshness, whatever kind is grown, should be the aim. Among the round cabbages, some good ones are Stonehead, Emerald Cross and Topper. There is usually a large number of entrants, consequently such classes are worth winning.

Cabbage Root Fly

One of the great problems with cauliflowers and cabbages that mature in August, is the root fly whose maggots attack the roots, making them look as though they are suffering from 'finger and toe disease'. One way to check the ravages is to dust around the necks immediately after planting out with 4 per cent calomel dust. It has a deterrent effect both upon the fly and finger and toe (clubroot). Another safeguard is to make discs or squares from black polythene (such as sedge peat comes in), dip them in Jeyes' Fluid and fit one around each plant.

Savoy and Red Cabbage

Savoys are sometimes exhibited in late shows. Other classes are for red pickling cabbage. Both take considerably more time to develop. In all respects they are cabbages, but unless specifically invited, they should never be staged as alternatives to the standard varieties.

Brussels Sprouts

Now and again there are classes for Brussels sprouts in late shows. For these, the best chances of gaining main awards are by exhibiting smallish hard closely folded sprouts, rather than large loosely packed ones. They are not worth growing in any special way. It is just a matter of getting the right varieties.

LETTUCES

Quite often there are classes for lettuces, and they are most useful if the schedule includes a collection of salads. There are seldom many entrants, and if they can be grown moderately well an attempt should be made to produce some specimens at whatever time of the year the show is held.

Of the cos and the cabbage types, there are variations of each – particularly the cabbage sort. There are 'butterhead' and 'crisp heart' varieties. While the former are of the better quality, they do not stand the test of showing during summer and autumn like the crisp hearts. Undoubtedly, the best crisp heart is Webb's Wonderful. It is most reliable and does produce lovely hearts that the judges can put their hands around approvingly. If there is a class for a cos variety, the one to grow is Jobjoits Green.

For the production of good lettuces, the soil must have the three following features: it must be lightish and contain plenty of humus; have a sufficient lime content; be consistently moist. Sow where the plants are to develop, taking care to thin out the seedlings very drastically rather than attempting to transplant. Guard against slugs, and malathion should be used as a safeguard against greenfly. Cut them as late as possible before the show, leaving just a little section of the taproots and removing any damaged outer leaves. Once you get them on the show bench, cut through the main roots as close to the best outer leaves, and place them flat on their bottoms if of the cabbage kind. Cos can only be placed on their sides.

SPINACH

Although spinach does not belong to the brassicas, it is a form of greenstuff and is occasionally exhibited, but from the cultivator's point of view it is hardly worth the effort to grow unless for home consumption. There are several variations of it, such as New Zealand with small leaves, and spinach beet with large thick foliage. The true spinach is raised from either round-seed or prickly varieties. The summer crops are invariably from round-seeded varieties of which there are several such as Sigmaleaf, King of Denmark and Reliance. When gathering, do so at the last minute and keep as much stalk as possible. Arrange the leaves on a largish plate in a rosette fashion, putting the best ones uppermost.

9

Fruiting Vegetables

TOMATOES

Tomatoes are so universally grown that it is hardly necessary to deal with their cultivation in this book, for everyone is acquainted with the various methods by which they are produced. Nevertheless, in order to win in usually hotly contested classes, it is necessary to have them just that little bit better than the rest.

The two chief factors are choosing the right varieties and growing them so that the plants are producing their best fruits on the important day. Timing is of the utmost importance in all forms of showing.

The majority of hybrids bred for the commercial growers are not the best for the gardener, either for eating or showing. The commercial men need fruits that will travel without bruising, whereas the gardener can cultivate those with more tender skins. The market growers usually gather the fruits when just starting to change colour from green, whereas we prefer to gather them when they have become almost ripe. The shopkeeper prefers them to be of smallish to medium size, in order to make the weighing easier, whereas we prefer them to be more sizeable, but not too large. There are some very large varieties, such as Big Boy, that are positively coarse. We need quality. The fruits should be shapely, look

c   65

bright and smooth, and have fresh-looking calyces that must always be revealed upon the show bench.

So far, the very best variety that I have grown for this purpose, and for home consumption, is Alicante. The shape is right, its condition perfect, and if given the necessary potash it ripens evenly over every part of the skin, with no trace whatever of greenback. Ailsa Craig is a very good variety, of long standing with a reputation for quality. It is worth growing for dual purposes; if showing, it is a good idea to put a label naming the variety on the dish, for this immediately makes a good impression upon the judges.

To gather and select my fruits for showing, I begin to gather the most likely looking specimens a week before the event. Those that have half changed colour and are of good even size and shape are gathered a week before the show and placed in a box in a cool room. Each day for the next four or five days others are gathered and treated similarly. The evening before the show, all are brought out and the requisite number, plus a fruit or two, are selected and carefully placed in a chip basket in tissue in readiness for carrying to the venue. The points to aim for are evenness of size, evenness of colour, freshness of calyces, and firmness. Very ripe soft specimens that have gone to a deep colour are despised. An occasional judge may prefer them, but the majority will reject over-ripeness. Some even give the fruits a pinch to cause a broken skin.

Generally, if tomato plants are grown in a greenhouse that is kept warm on cold nights until the end of May and is thereafter unheated, the best time to sow is the end of February. I also make another sowing in late March, so having a continuation of cropping for the home. As is generally known, it is important to feed with a potash fertiliser specially concocted for this fruit. It is possible to obtain larger fruits by reducing the numbers of each truss, but is hardly worth the effort; I prefer to have a large selection of fruits to choose from. Size can sometimes be a drawback if shape is wrong.

In some village shows there are special classes for 'outdoor grown'. The schedule really means just that, although the plants are first raised inside. They have to be grown in the open from the planting-out time. Usually these varieties look a bit tougher and more weatherworn than the indoor crops. The varieties for indoor culture produce better fruit than those 'bush' varieties specially offered for hardiness. Both Ailsa Craig and Alicante will grow outdoors during most summers. In case of a wet season, perhaps it is advisable to have both types.

Now and again, one finds in village schedules a class for the 'biggest truss of tomatoes'. It is not weight that determines the award as much as the length of the truss and the number of fruits it contains. When there are both weight and numbers the judges are pleased.

CUCUMBERS

I have grown tomatoes and cucumbers together in the same greenhouse and gained prizes for both, but it is not a very good thing to do if it is possible to have them in separate buildings. Whereas the tomato loves fresh air and plenty of sunshine, the cucumber prefers moisture and closeness and some shading. You all know the conditions this fruit needs. Firstly, a pile of manure, covered with soil – preferably John Innes No. 1. You plant the seedlings (which have been reared in a small pot) on the top, then train the main shoot up a cane until it reaches the apex of the roof or a height of 4 ft ($1 \cdot 2$ m), whichever is the shorter. At that height you pinch out the growing tip. There have to be horizontal wires or supports, not too near the glass, to which the sideshoots can be tied with raffia as they grow.

Eventually, flowers appear on these shoots, some being male and others female. These are distinguished by the female flowers having the embryo fruits immediately behind

67

them. You should not allow pollination to take place, but pick off the male flowers directly they have formed. Pollination spoils the shapes of the fruits, apart from making them bitter. The end of the sideshoot should be pinched out at the third leaf beyond where the fruit forms. After that further growths will spring from the sideshoots and it becomes a matter of discreet pinchings so that there follows a steady crop of fruits, amid a fair amount of foliage and stems. Too much pinching-out reduces the vigour of the plants. Likewise, leaving too much leafage and too many fruits impairs cropping and size.

It is unwise to be in too much of a hurry in the sowing of the seed for this crop. It needs considerable warmth for germination, which is quick if moisture and heat are forthcoming. You can, if conditions are favourable, allow twelve weeks between sowing and show date. It takes about a fortnight from the time of flowering until the fruits are ready to cut. The shrivelled blossom should remain at the growing end of the cucumber throughout, and kept intact when shown. Incidentally, I've known smart exhibitors who have fastened the dead blossom back again when it has become detached. I prefer to take it with me, and place it on the table, making it look as though it had dropped off while staging.

About an inch of stem is left on the fruit when cut. The exhibit should be handled with the utmost care, it being a defect if the natural 'bloom' of the skin is rubbed off. The colour should be deep green. For showing, the very best variety is Telegraph Improved. There are other varieties, such as Butcher's Disease Resisting, that are not as shapely, and there are now several varieties that bear all female flowers, thus making it unnecessary to pick off the males. But they do not come up to the standard of Telegraph Improved, either in smoothness, shape, or colour.

Cucumbers are prone to several rather distressful diseases but, if grown carefully, they seldom appear in small gardens. At least, that has been my experience.

Ridge Cucumbers

There are occasional classes for ridge cucumbers that must be grown outdoors. The best way to grow them is to make beds outdoors and sow direct in late May under cloches, removing these immediately the plants begin to grow in earnest. The new Japanese hybrids are excellent both for eating and showing. They produce few or no male flowers, thus failing to spoil the fruits. They are practically all hybrids, about the best being Tasty Green.

The time to gather fruits for showing should be when they appear to have fully developed. Judges look for evenness in a pair, length, fullness of the body, and tenderness, as well as the dead flower still remaining at the tip. With ridge cucumbers they invariably push their thumbnails into the necks or 'handles' of the fruits to check for tenderness. If the skin is hard to penetrate they shake their heads. I strive to get a similarity in the pair by cutting one when it has reached its perfection, two or three days before the show, and if the other is not quite long enough, let it remain until the last moment, if necessary, to complete its growth.

MARROWS

Apart from the heaviest marrow which is a joke class, it is rather a gamble to produce the best pair in a serious compeition, for it is generally a well-supported class – yet there are so many who enter who are terrific optimists. Chief qualities are evenness, tenderness, limit of a foot in length, good even colour and freshness.

Marrows should be mature, as well as being tender. Quite often one sees a long narrow anaemic pair that are insipid. It is advisable to grow a variety which will have all the desired qualities. Green Bush-Smallpak or Green Bush Improved are good.

69

Marrows like plenty of humus, lots of sunshine and shelter from wind. Water copiously in dry weather and syringe occasionally. The perforated triple hose placed over the plants and turned on for half an hour in the evenings after hot sunny days does them a lot of good. Once fruiting becomes heavy, feed with a liquid fertiliser. Pollinate the first female flowers, but cease once fruits begin to form.

As with cucumbers, in order to get a uniform pair you can cut the most suitable specimen two or three days before a show and look out for others to grow into conformity during the interval, or it may be possible to have just the right ones ready the day before. Cut with about 2 in (5 cm) of stem.

If you wish to produce the largest marrow, the variety Long Green is best. It is a trailer, and the growing tip has to be pinched out after the growth has made 3 ft (90 cm) or so. Once you are sure that three or four fruits are developing, you cull out all but the most promising specimen. Keep well watered and syringed.

Courgettes, the smaller marrows which are picked when around 7 in in length, have become increasingly popular but at the time of writing they are not included in show schedules.

PUMPKINS

In recent years, the pumpkin has become a popular subject in some districts, there being keen competition to produce the heaviest when all are judged at a venue (usually an inn) by invitation on a day in late autumn. The record for an individual fruit exceeds 200 pounds (91 kilos). To obtain anything near this weight involves remarkable skill, obtaining special seeds, and lots of luck. Manure, sunshine, water, etc, are essential in proportionate quantities, and plants are allowed to produce only one fruit each. Once they begin to swell, the chief concern is to keep them growing rather than letting them get to a ripening stage. Small doses of saltpetre gives them a fillip.

SWEET CORN

This is an increasingly popular vegetable both for edible and for show purposes. It is not much help in a collection, but if to be grown for show (as well as for consumption), it should be noted that varieties are much improving year by year. Most are hybrids. The largest, such as Kelvedon Glory, are usually too late for August shows. At the moment, the one most favoured is John Innes F1.

A sheltered position and deeply dug ground (without manure) are the chief demands. Plant seeds, individually, in small pots during early May, and raise in cool greenhouse. Plant out in the last days of May, after the frosts have (hopefully) finished, spacing them 18 in (45 cm) apart, preferably in blocks rather than rows to assist pollination. Put them slightly deeper than when in the pots. Provide canes if this seems necessary, although they should not be required if the position is well sheltered.

The cobs have green sheaths with tassels at the growing ends. When these tassels (sometimes called silks) turn to a deep brown colour, ripening begins. When preparing for show, the sheath can be gently pulled away, exposing the grain throughout. If you have a choice, select those cobs that have the best overall appearance, with no gaps in the rows of grain. They should be firm rather than soft or hard, and look exceedingly fresh. When staging it is better to put them upon a suitable plate than merely to lay them on the tabling.

Flower Collections

While I personally take much pride in obtaining prizes for vegetables, I derive more pleasure from gaining the main awards for collections of hardy perennials and of annuals, whether the latter are hardy or not. These are quite distinct from the competitions amongst the specialists of the grand florists, flowers such as super chrysanthemums, dahlias, roses, sweet peas, and the like. Those individual subjects generally are too time-consuming, and to grow them exceedingly well has to be at the expense of the other occupants of the garden.

To stage the best collection of half a dozen distinct sorts of perennials gives considerable scope and attracts the passer-by, for they are subjects more in keeping with things they grow themselves. It is much the same with annuals, whether these be hardy or grown from seeds grown under glass, so causing them to be described as 'half-hardy'. There are three forms of skill needed – choosing the most suitable varieties, growing them properly, and preparing them for showing.

When determining what to grow it is best not to be clever, but to rely upon good tested varieties rather than try to impress with novelties. Also, be sure that the flowers you enter conform strictly to the classification. You always meet people who like to reveal their own adroitness, such as including in perennials shrubs like buddleias because they bear flowers year after year. However, to the judges they are shrubs. Again, these people will show pentstemons, or antirrhinums, insisting they are perennial – which they are – but as most are raised the same year, they are more annual than otherwise. But they are bad annuals too, so unless there are special classes for them it is best not to include suchlike in your collections. There are plenty of hardy perennials, and annuals, to choose from without risking controversy.

When I am judging such classes I check whether the rules and regulations included in the schedule make any reference to such problem flowers. If they do not, I pass such flowers by if there are other good entries that are truly representative, and about which there are no doubts.

PERENNIALS

If you wish to grow true perennials most likely to be good for cutting and showing during the month of August, the following are some of the best:

Achillea filipendulina 'Gold Plate'
Aconitum 'Arendsii'
Artemisia lactiflora
Campanula 'Prichard's Variety'
Eryngium variifolium
Helenium 'Wyndley'
Helianthus 'Loddon Gold'
Heliopsis 'Goldgreenheart'
Lythrum virgatum 'Rose Queen'
Phlox paniculata 'Brigadier'
Rudbeckia 'Autumn Sun'
Sidalcea 'Croftway Red'
Solidago 'Golden Shower'
Solidaster luteus

Thalictrum dipterocarpum 'Hewitt's Double'
Veronica exaltata

In some instances there are several varieties that can be considered equally with those named, especially among Japanese anemones, phloxes, heleniums, rudbeckias, sidalceas and solidagos.

There are also other herbaceous flowers I have not mentioned that sometimes make a good show in August, but cannot be relied upon to do so, one such being *Primula florindae* which has been used with startling effect. *Scabiosa* 'Clive Greaves' makes a beautiful vase, but there are seldom enough flowers open at one time and it is fatal to include any whose centres have blown.

Although there may be better methods of presenting collections of perennials at flower shows I have my own ways of doing so, and have found they suit the flowers as well as myself. During the afternoon of the day preceding the show I gather each sort of flower, one by one – take, for example the Japanese anemones. As many blooms as are wanted are cut, with considerable length of stem, and carried to the flower room. Here they are laid on a table, and then each stem is taken singly to have the lower leaves stripped off to about halfway. I then take a sharp knife and shorten the stem by cutting off a piece at a very sharp angle, not straight across. This is to avert the formation of air bubbles. That done, the bloom is placed in a bucket or container of water up to the level of the leaves, the latter being kept just clear. The rest of the collection are gathered in turn and treated in exactly the same way. It pays to make as many journeys to the garden as there are bunches needed. If the collection is to be of six sorts, if possible I obtain eight so that there is a choice.

Even with the use of the oblique cut, now and again a perennial will flop – one such being the helianthus. That bloom will not be taken to the show. The majority will look much more perky and fulsome than they did in the garden.

FLOWER COLLECTIONS

In the morning, at the last moment, the different kinds are
tied into separate bunches and packed together in a long box,
lined with newspaper, or put into a suitable basket. Upon
arrival at the show the vases are brought out and each is half
filled with water. Then the bunches are undone, and in turn
put into the respective vases, stem by stem. As each bloom
is lifted from its bunch it is held upside down and given a
brisk shake. This shapes up the foliage and the flowers and
causes any tired petals to fall off, which does happen with
phlox although it is unlikely with Japanese anemones. Each
stem is then shortened, if necessary, to the right height for
the vase, and any defects are snipped off as well. When
placed in the vase a nice oval effect should be aimed at for
bunchy flowers like campanulas, phlox, rudbeckias and
sucklike; in the case of solidago, artemisia or monkshood,
the spikes should be well balanced, showing no gaps but each
appearing to be essential to the others. Make the vases
fulsome, but never overcrowd. Many an exhibitor has lost
through overcrowding, especially when using inferior heads
of flowers to make up bulk.

Having decided on the positioning of the vases, taking into
consideration heights, shapes, colours and contrasts, you
complete by topping up with water. Vases with widish tops,
narrow waists and broad bases are best. I prefer earthenware, although there are metal and plastic containers
available. They should be opaque.

With some flowers that are difficult to keep in position,
you can put into the vases some pieces of coiled-up wire
netting. There should just be enough to keep the stems in
position. If the mesh is too small you cannot get the stems
in place without upsetting the flowers you have already
inserted. You may use pieces of foliage to camouflage the
netting but only leaves of the type of flower exhibited. Care
should be taken about this. Flowers with bare stems, such
as scabious, must stand out sharp and clear. Only scabious
leaves tucked in around the neck of the vase can be used. The

whole exercise is to make the flowers look as natural as possible, and let nothing detract.

ANNUALS

As already advised, it is no use arguing whether an antirrhinum is an annual or a perennial. Other flowers in this dubious category are scarlet salvias, carnations, petunias, gazanias, heliotropes, lobelias and pentstemons.

There are some judges as well as competitors who like to reveal their pedantic knowledge, and the best way to beat them is to never give them a chance to show it. Annuals that *are* annuals and nothing more, can never be disputed. However, whether a certain flower is tender, half-hardy, or completely hardy can sometimes lead to argument. If a schedule simply states that a class is for a given number of 'annuals', I regard the following as being the best:

African marigolds	Six-weeks stocks
China aster	Salpiglossis
Nicotiana	Zinnia

Large-flowered tall varieties are always preferable, for not only are the individual flowers pronounced, the stems allow for impressive heights. Those six can be regarded as half-hardy subjects, therefore ineligible in a class where 'hardy annuals' is specified.

Among the best in the latter class are:

Calendula	Larkspur
Centaurea moschata	Lavatera
(sweet sultan)	Nigella
Clarkia	Saponaria
Godetia	

The stems of annuals are fleshier and softer than those of perennials and most take water easily, therefore it is less essential to cut them obliquely. I like to use a pair of scissors or very sharp secateurs. The best procedure is to carry pails half-filled with water to where the flowers are growing. If the weather is fine this job is left until the evening of the day before the show, but if wetness prevails (which is too often) plastic sheeting is suspended over the beds two days before, and the flowers are gathered in the morning of the day before showing, taking great care when putting them in the pails or containers so that the heads do not touch one another. This can be ensured by putting crumpled large-mesh wire netting into the container, into which the stems can be threaded after removing the lower leaves, any side-buds unlikely to open and any faded blossoms. On the day of the show the blooms are tied together in small bunches, using raffia, and placed in shallow flat baskets, or stood in the containers from which most of the water has been tipped out.

Vases need not be as large as those for perennials. They should be of similar shape, i.e., widish tops, thin waists and broad bases, so that they do not topple when staged. Half fill with water before putting in the blooms, and then top up when you have finally positioned them. Try to get every vase of flowers similar in size, rather than make a grand show of something just because you have a lot of it. You cannot blind the judges by bulk unless all are bulky, and even then it may be a drawback. Make your display so that every flower or spike of flowers is exhibited fully, and if pulled out leaves a gap. The judges are looking for quality, evenness, and freedom from blemishes. Annuals are cleaner and fresher than perennials. If you have a lovely vase of flowers not as tall as the others, you should raise it by placing a block of wood or covered brick under the base. This is a good idea if it can be done without being conspicuous.

At one time, show tabling was very rough and often dirty, but in recent years there has been an improvement, with organisers covering the surface with cloth or paper. However, be prepared for all eventualities and have sheets of matt white paper available to lay over the tabling if it needs it.

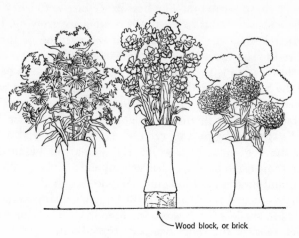

Wood block, or brick

7. Displaying annuals

My comments so far have been about unspecified 'vases' of annuals, but there are often several classes of specific annuals, asking for a certain number of blooms – for instance, six asters, or marigolds, or zinnias. There are certain things to mind and heed when competing in such classes as these. Only recently I was disqualified in a class for six marigolds simply because I had used marigold foliage to pack the vase, instead of wire netting. This would have been all right but for the fact that on one of the stems I used there was a very small bud. The judges regarded this as a prospective flower, therefore I was showing more than the stipulated number. It was a ridiculous situation to say the least. However, I accepted the decision with good grace, although I would never have made such a one myself. So take care – never include in foliage a vestige of a bud where a limited number of individual flowers has to be shown.

Also, take heed of such wording as 'one variety only'. In that case never show a mixture of colours. If showing mari-

78

golds, of which there are lemon and gold, either have one or the other. I think that, where there are no such rules, to have six blooms all the same size, shape and colour is likely to pull the award, rather than a mixture, particularly if the colours and sizes of the latter are unbalanced.

I I

Chrysanthemums

By adopting special systems of cultivation, including the control of light, it is possible to have chrysanthemums throughout the year. But the normal flowering season is November when large specimens are grown for competitions held throughout Britain, and in other countries too. Most of them are organised by local specialist societies that are affiliated to national or international organisations, and one must be a member in order to be a completely successful exhibitor, for the rules, regulations, innumerable new varieties, and methods of growing are constantly being changed, and it is difficult to keep up to date without becoming a subscriber. A general indication of the demands of this class of flower is all that I can offer here.

However, at the August flower shows there are usually classes for early flowering blooms and it is not so difficult to be among the winners. Whereas, practically throughout their lives, the November flowers are grown in containers, these August varieties will grow into lovely blossoms in the open garden during late spring and summer.

Although chrysanthemums are perennials they are, for show purposes at least, propagated afresh each winter from cuttings taken off the old roots. After the flowers have faded the stems are cut down to within three or four inches (7·5 or 10 cm) of the base, and the plants, if late varieties, are kept in their pots, generally in a cold frame or cool greenhouse. Beyond keeping them moist and free from frost, they must remain as cool as possible. The early flowering ones are, after their season, lifted from the garden and planted closely together in boxes or frames, and given the identical conditions of the late-flowerers.

Early Flowering

During January and February the indoor types throw up suckers around the old stems. The outdoor varieties, strangely enough, send theirs up later. They are severed from below the soil surface with a sharp knife when about 3 in (7·5 cm) high. These 'cuttings' are then trimmed by being cut through again at the base immediately below an apparent joint in the stem, and the lower leaves are removed (a razor blade is the best thing to use for this). They are inserted in a bed of sandy compost which can be spread over the staging in the cool greenhouse, or in a box, or, if only a few are needed, an ordinary 5-in (12-cm) clay pot.

I like striking (rooting) chrysanthemums in clay pots. The usual mixture is one part sterilised loam, one part soaked sphagnum peat and two parts sharp sand. After putting in crocks for drainage and filling almost to the top with the mixture, the cuttings are inserted around the inside

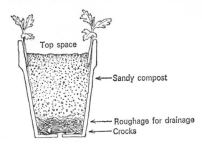

8. *Striking chrysanthemum cuttings*

close up to the hard clay, putting the ends in to the depth of about an inch. Either one or three more cuttings are inserted in the centre of the pot, just to fill up the space. They are watered in and then stood in a temperature of around 7°C (45°F). A spray when the air is dry is all the attention they get.

Some growers put their cuttings in a propagator, consisting of wooden sides and glass top, to conserve the atmosphere. Others use hormone powders as well. While I do not regard these as necessary under my conditions, they may be beneficial in other circumstances such as a dry warm greenhouse. However, when kept in too close an atmosphere in a propagator there is a risk of 'damping off'.

Rooting has taken place when the cuttings begin to grow. You then put each one into a small flower pot, using a soil mixture such as John Innes No. 1 and perhaps adding a little peat to soften it for the tender roots. Kept cool and protected, the young plants grow quickly. Directly the roots have filled the pots the plants are transferred into a 5-in (12-cm) size and grown on, still keeping as cool as possible, just free from frost all the time. By the end of March they are ready to go into the cold frame, where they can be given air during nice weather and only covered at night, or the glass-light put over when there is excessive rain. By the time to plant out, the first week of May being good for this, they are quite hardy and experience hardly any check unless the roots are upset.

The site is prepared during winter. Well-decayed manure is dug in deeply and bonemeal is also forked in. Left until the end of April, the bed is forked through again and stakes are inserted one at every place where a plant will go. Good distances are $1\frac{1}{2}$ ft (45 cm) apart within the rows, placing the matter $2\frac{1}{2}$ ft (75 cm) distant.

Disbudding

Having planted your chrysanthemums in the garden they then need to have the top growths pinched out to encourage them to develop branches. Most times, four is a nice number – the rest sprouting from the axils of the leaves are pinched out. Those four are tied individually to the stake as seems necessary, somewhat loosely, but closely enough to stop them swaying heavily in the wind.

In due course, they form flower buds at the extremities – a considerable number of them. All but the strongest one on each stem are picked off while quite small, so that the vigour is concentrated in the remaining one.

Bloom Protection

The next task is to protect the bud from the weather. For this there are special bloom protector frames available in various sizes and forms. One type is a wire framework that is attached to the stake, over which a bag is drawn. Care is needed in putting these in position, and they should not be applied before the buds are showing colour. They are then left for about twelve days, after which they are removed and the open flower cut with plenty of stem. A firm specialising in supplying showmen with these appliances as well as special fertilisers for both early outdoor and late indoor chrysanthemums is Joseph Bentley Limited, Barrow-on-Humber DN19 7AQ. One important point about these protector bags is that they must be left on the blooms until the last moment. You spoil the flowers if you inspect during the interim. Some protector bags are fitted with windows through which you can peep to satisfy your curiosity or detect any problems. One sensible precaution is to spray the flower head with an insecticide before covering.

You cannot control the time of flowering of early outdoor chrysanthemums with any degree of success. The only way to ensure that you have a choice of blooms at the right time is to grow varieties that are reputed to arrive when you want them. If, for instance, your show is to be held on 12th August, then you obtain every specialist catalogue you can and select the names of those varieties that are marked 'mid-August.' By studying all the catalogues and making comparisons, not only can you get some degree of accuracy, but also obtain a fair idea of which are the best varieties. It generally pays to ignore specialists' expensive novelties – only when a newcomer appears in several lists is it worth experimenting with.

If you propagate your own plants from cuttings reasonably well, they will most times be better than the young plants you buy. The nurserymen are churning them out by the thousand, often raising them in warmer conditions than is good for them, and when they arrive it pays to repot and keep them a while in the greenhouse or frame before putting them in the open ground. However, as new varieties are coming along all the time, one has to get a few in order to propagate from them in the following years.

Late Flowering

As already stated, the November-flowering plants need considerably more skill and lots more attention. One has to be completely dedicated in order to get them to the high pitch of perfection obtained by top competitors. Having raised them from cuttings and potted them on in the greenhouse, much as described for the early flowering ones, instead of being planted in the garden they are put into large pots, the final potting being done in early June. Once that is carried out, they are placed outdoors, preferably on an ash bed, although I've put hundreds of them along one side of a wide gravel path. Each pot has its main stake which is attached securely to a strand of wire held in position by strong posts inserted in the ground. This wire is suspended about 4 ft (1·2 m) from ground level and held taut, so that winds do not blow over the pots. If necessary, two strands of wire are used.

Each day they have to be watered, sometimes twice or thrice when the weather is sunny and dry. They have to be given fertilisers occasionally, and be sprayed against all manner of pests. When first potted there is generally enough room left for top-dressings to be applied as deemed necessary.

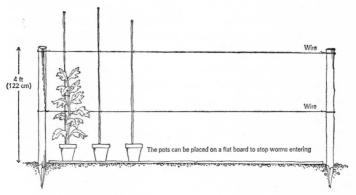

9. *Late flowering chrysanthemums*

Stopping and Disbudding

These tasks can be complicated. By adopting certain tactics it is possible to have blossoms in season for a particular show (as distinct from early flowering kinds). The experts have their own jargon. In this case the catalogues will tell you to take 'first-crown-buds', 'second-' or 'third-crown-buds' according to variety. It means that you first of all stop, or pinch out, the top to encourage branching – when a bud forms at the top, you remove it so that another side-

85

shoot appears below and grows up until it, in its turn, forms a bud. Still again, in some instances, you remove that bud to cause another side growth to appear and in its turn produce a bud at the top. This is known as a 'terminal', and is the one allowed to open into a flower. In the course of this exercise, the plants produce a large number of shoots, all of which have to be removed except the ones you elect to grow – also the many other, unwanted, buds are rubbed off so that all the concentrated energy goes into those wonderful blossoms you hope to produce.

These show chrysanthemums are classified into many sections and one needs to be a flower lawyer in order to be correct. There are large exhibition, medium exhibition, decorative, pompon, anemone-flowered, single, exhibition incurved, reflexed decoratives, etc, etc. With the aid of specialists' catalogues and books compiled by the experts, one can in time get a general idea of the differences, and probably end up by concentrating upon one section such as the single varieties that are the easiest for beginners.

Pests and Diseases

Chrysanthemums are subject to many pests and diseases. A vigilant attitude must be kept all the time. Some bothers are contagious, among these being eelworm which lives on the outside of the plants and turns the foliage black. Other pests are aphids, leaf miners, midges, caterpillars and earwigs. Chief diseases are mildew and viruses. There is an ever-creasing number of antidotes for all these troubles, and those who grow late-flowering chrysanthemums should be familiar with them. Happily, most of these nuisances seldom attack the chrysanthemums we grow in the garden for the August shows. However, they are not completely immune and the grower must always be on the alert.

Showing

Chrysanthemum flowers are notoriously prone to flop after cutting. The woody stems develop air bubbles, so stopping the absorption of water upwards. One way to control this nuisance is to first of all cut the stem low down when removing from the plant, strip off some of the lower leaves and then place it in a deepish pail of water. Now cut the stem through again while holding it under the water – this prevents the bubble forming the second time. Having soaked the stems for a few hours, you then lift them out one by one, and with a very sharp knife you cut them through once more, obliquely, at the same time making a slit upwards about an inch (2·5 cm) in length, before putting into the show vase.

You need vases with broad bases to hold the flowers, and they should be of good size. Having slit your stems it is rather difficult to use wire netting to keep them upright, as advocated for the perennials and annuals. I find that suitable pieces of privet with all foliage removed, or unwanted chrysanthemum stems, when pushed into a vase will form a wedge at the bottom and allow enough room at the top into which the flower stems can be inserted and 'packed' with more pieces of bare stem in order to hold them in position, with their heads in pleasing formation, kept distinctly apart, yet not having large gaps between.

The chief qualities which judges look for are depth of bloom, shape of bloom, similarity, and whether the flowers conform to the classification. The petals should be perfect throughout, any stained or faded being drawbacks. If reflexed petals are called for they must surely be reflexed. Likewise, incurved should be compact and forming a ball, each tip being rounded. It is inadvisable to pluck off bad petals, especially those at the back. If they are not too badly affected, I have often judiciously trimmed the tarnished edges with a pair of sharp scissors, and with a light pair of tweezers carefully adjusted any petals not conforming to the general pattern. If there are blemishes they are the first things the judges see, but if you have carefully removed them without plucking out any leaves and carefully adjusted the petals, you can often gain an award which you wouldn't otherwise do.

12

Dahlias

All who aspire to prominence in local shows should cultivate dahlias; they not only provide a colourful display which attracts a lot of attention, they are comparatively easy to produce. In most flower shows there are classes for all sections of the community, and if you are an amateur you can compete as such, as well as pit your skill against the experts in the 'open' section. Furthermore, if you are a member of the local organisation, quite often there are special classes for you as well. In addition to winning the prizes in their classes, they also help to tot up the points for the cups that most societies present to their champions.

In our local society's schedule there are eight classes for dahlias, spread among the sections that are restricted or open to all. They are for four types: firstly the decoratives, secondly the cactus or semi-cactus, thirdly the pompons, and lastly the class for the best single specimen of any kind. This is usually a gigantic decorative with masses of broad petals, but it can be a cactus, or semi-cactus, should you happen to have a good one.

The first essential is getting the right varieties. We have to be sure that our flowers are really of the decorative class, or whatever, and not those of another classification. The way to make sure is to obtain as many specialists' catalogues as possible and peruse them intelligently. Most of them are accurate and reliable, and, incidentally, often contain valuable information about the individual flowers, as well as giving hints on cultivation.

When choosing, it is best to ignore the most expensive novelties – that is, unless one already has a collection of trusted ones, and is merely adding a new name just for experiment. By studying the available lists, one soon becomes familiar with the titles of the most popular varieties, although these need not necessarily be the best for exhibition purposes. By study, it is possible to distinguish which are which.

Generally, in the case of the decorative and the cactus varieties, it pays to grow those which produce the larger blossoms. While a few judges are expert dahlia growers, the majority of them are general gardeners who are inclined, other things being equal, to favour size and brightness of colour.

In the special autumn shows there may be – in fact, more often are – classes for large, medium and small varieties of the decorative and the medium groups. And in larger shows there are also giant and miniature varieties in both instances. However, unless one is prepared to cultivate dahlias in a big way, such extreme interest is best deferred.

POMPONS

A class of dahlia that appeals to me more than any other is the pompon. It generally specifies five (or six) blooms, either of one colour or mixed, leaving you the option. Most schedules stipulate that no blossom shall exceed 2 in (5 cm) in diameter. It is the one class that causes more disappointments or gives the most pleasure.

I have been a judge at shows where as many as half a dozen exhibitors have not obeyed the rule regarding diameter – one or more bloom in each vase having been too large. It gave the judges a headache, for when all are breaking the rules what can one do?

The way to make sure of the correct size is to fit yourself up with a 2-in (5-cm) gauge. To make it yourself, get a round piece of wood precisely 2 in (5 cm) in diameter and wind round it a piece of pliant but stiffish wire, twisting the ends into shape for use as a handle – now remove the block of wood. By passing the ring over each flower you can be sure that none exceed the 2-in (5-cm) limit, while all should practically fill the gauge. Be sure that the varieties are true pompon, and not 'ball' dahlias, nor miniature varieties of any other group. In other words, be sure your flowers are true to classification. Pompon dahlias are globular; the petals fold inwards and are blunt-ended.

There are specialists in the pompon group who cultivate many scores of varieties, exchanging them with other enthusiasts in other parts of the world, especially Australia, while Belgium, Sweden and Germany also have many growers. In local shows, you are just as likely to find blooms as good as any of them.

One of the problems of selecting dahlias is that some come into flower earlier than others. As flower shows are most times held before the dahlias reach their zenith, it is well to get those that are reputed to be early. On this account, and also the fact that some behave according to the weather, it is best to have several varieties, rather than a lot of plants of a few types.

While new ones are often boosted, especially in the pompon group, and there are hundreds of colours or combinations of shades, just for a limited number the most promising ones are those that are dark red or lavender.

CACTUS

In the case of cactus or semi-cactus varieties, the majority come into flower earlier than is the case with other groups. Some of the semi-cactus types have petals that are not as quilled as they should be. While experts will know them, the ordinary judge will often ponder as to whether the blooms are really cactus, or almost of the decorative class. This is a point to bear in mind when buying varieties for local competitions, as against competing with the specialists.

Among the old and trusted large cactus varieties are Berkey, lemon-yellow shaded orange-pink; Drakenburg, salmon tinged with mauve, orange and violet; Encore, yellow; Nutley Surprise, a mixture of pink, orange and rose; and Polar Sight, white. However, these are being superseded by new introductions. A bloom from one of these can often be staged for that 'one specimen dahlia'. The whopper decorative specimen is most often entered, but it can be a drawback if too floppy or having the slightest defect.

The annual number of new varieties in the decorative group is bewildering – you should regard them critically. So many are inferior to those that have passed the test of time, and many are quite good florists but useless on the exhibition table. In this connection, the 'water-lily decorative' type should be avoided, one example being 'Gerrie Hoek' which has insufficient petals and is too shallow for our purpose.

Wherever you go, where dahlias are grown, look upon them appraisingly. Apart from colour, which should be paramount, some have defects, such as weak stems or nodding heads. All blooms should have their 'chins up'.

Beware of varieties that have greenish cores in the centres of the blooms. While this fault may be due to wrong cultivation, in most instances it is a varietal weakness.

When you attend national shows where there are stands of these most attractive, from the point of view of colour, of all flowers, ask the attendants about times of flowering and whether they make large tubers or not – for unless they do, and you wish to propagate from them, you may not be able to obtain cuttings. I never hesitate to elicit this information.

Cultivation

Dahlias are distributed in three different forms. Firstly there are the pot tubers that are normally put into packs and sold in shops, garden centres, etc. They generally have a picture on the front, showing what the contents should grow into. You buy these and plant in the garden in early May, or start them in a frostproof greenhouse during April, hardening-off and planting out at the end of May or early June. I don't like buying dahlias that way – there is a risk of their being infected with a virus, so causing them to produce inferior blooms. However, it is generally safe to buy tubers of this sort from a genuine specialist, for his stock should be free from such trouble.

In my opinion the best way to obtain dahlias, is to buy rooted cuttings, generally raised by the suppliers. These are usually sent out in April. Some are sold in May, but the latter do not grow into flowering plants in time for the early August shows. If you have a greenhouse, it is a great advantage to get these rooted cuttings as early as possible, plant them individually in small clay or plastic containers (not polythene or paper) and grow them on, eventually planting out in late May or early June.

There are many ways of lifting and storing dahlias during winter, and these are frequently described. To propagate from old stock other than by division, such as by taking one's own cuttings or producing pot tubers, can become an exacting pastime that has to be studied more assiduously than I can deal with in these notes.

The general methods of dahlia cultivation are given repeatedly in every journal, and demonstrated on the television screen every season. To reiterate the chief points, the old tubers can be planted outdoors in late April, the pot tubers during early May, and the rooted cuttings, or green plants, at the end of May or early June. Dahlias are very sensitive to frost and have to be properly hardened-off before being planted out, once they start to produce shoots.

The plants should be provided with supporting stakes. These should be substantial, preferably sawn inch-square pieces of wood about 5 ft (1·5 m) long, painted green with the lower sharpened ends treated with a preservative. Insert each one in the hole made for the plant (or close to it) before the latter is introduced. The best spacing is 2 ft 6 in (75 cm) apart, in rows that are 5 ft 6 in (165 cm) asunder.

The soil should be well drained and in good heart. Manure is best dug in during the previous autumn or used as a mulch after the plants are growing nicely. At the time of planting, scatter and fork in bonemeal at the rate of 2 oz (57 g) for each plant. Before planting get the roots thoroughly moist. After planting, do not water again until the ground around is obviously dry.

About a fortnight after planting, nip out the tip of the main shoot to encourage branching. At all times look out for pests. Slugs can be controlled by scattering a bait quite early on. As they grow, tie the individual shoots rather loosely to the stake. About every fortnight or so, spray the plants with an insecticide – this will prevent aphis infection and caterpillars. Derris is one of the best applications, but it does not control earwigs to any extent. The traditional small pot (in which hay or paper has been tucked) placed inverted on the stake is a great help. Hold the pot over a bucket of water while examining it for these pests.

Disbudding

Once the shoots beging to grow quickly they soon produce flower buds, most often three at a time, one being at the apex and the other two sprouting from the axils of a pair of leaves lower down the stem. It is best to remove the latter two buds so that all nourishment goes into the stem and flower at the extremity. Having produced the flower, further growths from the base of the branch will develop and in turn become branches if allowed to grow. In the case of pompons it is best to leave them unchecked, but in the cactus and decorative groups they may be too dense, so some of them are removed at the starting point. There will be enough left to produce an increasing number of beautiful and gay flowers until autumn frosts kill off the tops.

Protection

The next problem the show grower may meet is shading from hot sunshine during scorching weather, or protecting them from rain during bad times. When I want flowers for show I rig up fairly firm temporary shelters by knocking in posts, and putting over some polythene sheeting. One has to be careful that this form of protection does not do more harm than good, for if it chafes the plants, or falls upon them, it is disastrous. One only needs to keep the warmest sun, or the extreme wet off the blooms for a brief period before a show.

Showing

Flowers should be gathered in the early morning or the evening of the day preceding the show. The best procedure is to cut with a pair of sharp secateurs, having the stem as long as possible. Hold each cut end in a pail of water and cut through again. Carry the blooms in their container to a cool building and let them stay until the early morning. Pack them so that no blooms are damaged, and directly you get them to the show put them in water; before doing so, use a very sharp knife and cut about 2 in (5 cm) of the stem through at an oblique angle. Half fill your vases, put in supporting material – which can be loose wire-netting or stems of dahlias with foliage removed – and then cut once more with the knife at an angle if the stems need to be shortened to obtain perfect symmetry. However, it always pays to have as long stems as possible, so that the blooms stand up well among their competitors, each head facing the same way. Finally, top up the water.

Care should be taken to have specimens of the same varieties exactly similar. Should you find it difficult to obtain enough of any one variety to fill a vase of five it is wiser to use three of one type and two of another, rather than put in an odd one just to make up the number (which I've seen done). However, if you have an outstanding variety and enough even flowers they generally make more impact than a mixed lot.

Sometimes, one reads such rules as 'five cactus flowers, not less than three varieties'. You don't stand much chance if you put in three of one, and one each of two others. Better to have five separate varieties if you can find the quality and a degree of evenness.

I have purposely devoted considerable space to dahlias because of their importance in August shows, and their not being so very difficult from the cultivation angle.

13

Sweet Peas

There are very few sweet peas of quality exhibited in the August flower shows. They do not make a good vase display in collections of annuals, and their season has passed. They are at their best around midsummer and are often combined with roses for an event on the vicarage lawn, or some such festival.

There are sweet pea societies, both on a national and a local level, just as there are societies for chrysanthemums, dahlias and roses. If you want to become a show specialist, it is advisable to subscribe to such a society so that you can be familiar with the newest varieties and the latest hints on cultivation.

The seed doesn't cost much, but there must be an outlay on bamboos, up which to train the plants; but the chief requirements are time, patience and strength to attend to these beautiful flowers when grown on the single-stem system.

The first essential is to obtain your seed from a reliable specialist, rather than rely upon cheap offers or collections of varieties. Seldom does a collection, from whatever source, contain all the best ones. Only by studying the catalogues of several firms will you select the best assortment of winners. You ignore the boosted ones unless they are praised by all, and you also find out which varieties are most favoured by the experts.

To grow them the single-stem way involves, after preparation of the site, the erection of posts and cross-pieces
about 6 ft (1·8 m) high, to which are fastened two strands of
wire, like aerial masts; to these are fastened upright 8-ft
bamboo canes. It is a good plan to only obtain 7-ft canes and
instead of pushing their lower ends into the ground, insert
pieces of wood that project 6 in above the surface and fasten
the canes to these – this method saves the canes from perish-
ing. At the end of the season the pegs can be pulled out and
burned, while the canes can be cleaned and the ends dipped
in Cuprinol to preserve them for several seasons.

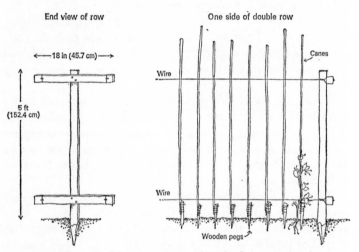

10 and 11. *Staking sweet peas for single stem-growing*

The site is prepared during autumn by deeply double
digging throughout, mixing in lots of well-decayed manure,
or compost, and some bonemeal. Some growers merely make
trenches where the rows are to go but this method is not as
good as double digging the whole plot throughout.

Seed and Seedlings

Seed is sown in boxes of light soil in late September or early October, January and February, and germinated in a cool greenhouse. Once growing, the boxes are transferred to a cold frame, where the plants can be kept well ventilated and exposed to the open air whenever the weather is congenial. They suffer more from excessive wetness than cold, but it pays to protect them from very severe frosts.

When three or four leaves have formed, the growing tip is pinched out, to encourage strong sideshoots to develop. All but the sturdiest of these are then nipped off so that all nourishment goes into the selected shoots, thus making a much stronger growth than if the initial leading shoot was retained.

The early-grown batch are most times potted off singly in January, putting them in the cool greenhouse for a few days after the operation, but soon placing them back in the cold frame. John Innes No. 1 Compost is a good mixture for this move.

In the south, the second week of April is a good time to plant the seedlings outdoors, putting each one at the base of the support inside the double line of canes; a few weeks later is better for colder districts. There are arguments whether to loosen out the longish roots, or keep them in the ball of soil as it comes out of the pot. I think it pays to scratch the surface of the ball carefully so that the roots can break through. Bought plants are generally without soil to save postage and packing – make each hole deep in that case, so that the lowest rootlets dangle down against the wall of soil; gently firm them in.

Training

The plants soon begin to grow and need to be supported by looping them to the canes. They will thereafter need constant attention, all growths from the axils of the leaves being picked out and the tendrils snipped off with a knife as soon as they appear. Also, embryo flower stems should be removed close to the vine until a height of about 4 ft (1·2 m) is reached. Only then should the plant be allowed to produce flowers.

By this time the plants are really strong and growing lustily, consequently the flower stems will come long and strong. These should be gathered regularly, and the nipping out of sideshoots and tendrils continued until the tops of the bamboo canes are reached. When this happens, all are released from the canes and either curled round into a clump, or laid along the surface one above the other so that the growing ends are trained to the canes afresh, starting all over again. If laid along the ground, for instance, the plant growing on No. 1 cane can be trained to now grow up No. 5, or even No. 6 and so on, training the end plants of the rows around to the other side.

Watering and Feeding

If the weather is dry the plants must be watered, rather copiously instead of in dribs and drabs. I find nothing better than perforated triple hose laid between the rows and left for a couple of hours. The water is then aerated, falls gently, and gives no shock to the roots. Peas suffer from shock if cold water is given in large quantities.

The plants also have to be fed. Various growers suggest various forms of this; some even advise the use of sulphate of ammonia, which is asking for trouble. I prefer to use the fertiliser sold by manufacturers specially for feeding to tomatoes. It contains considerable amounts of potash and can be applied when watering, or if it rains. Never give the plants food when the ground is dry. That hint applies to vegetation in general.

Pests and Diseases

Sweet peas are subject to several pests and diseases that are often transmitted by greenfly. If you see any plants with curling leaves look closely, and if necessary spray with a suitable insecticide. Mildew will attack the stems and foliage during damp periods after dry weather, and leaves will turn yellow in some gardens in some years. However, if one grows only for the summer shows, these troubles will not appear before those events have come and gone.

Showing

About two days before a show is due is the time to view your crop critically and decide upon those blooms you will take along, from which you will make your final selection. You always need more on hand than you will use for several reasons – bruising, lack of lustre or failure to open evenly. The last picking should be done on the morning preceding the show and every stem should have three open flowers while the topmost is on the verge of doing so. Placed in water it is surprising how much they will improve within a few hours – the half-open blossom extending to fullness and the others standing out full and proud of themselves.

It is not essential to steep them up to their necks. I prefer to put them in discarded instant coffee or Horlicks jars filled with water. They have the right depth and the right aperture to hold the stems correctly, especially if a little piece of wire netting is put in the base to keep the bottom of the stems in the right positions. The flowers should not touch each other and should be kept in an airy cool building overnight. In the morning they are taken from the jars carefully, the water shaken off the stems, and packed flat side by side in long flat boxes, and kept in position by crinkled newspaper. Directly upon arrival at the show they are put into deepish water again, so that they can then be arranged in the show vases as needed.

The vast majority of sweet pea exhibitors use special metal vases. These are very light, yet strong, and are so shaped that they show off the sweet peas in the best possible way. Each vase consists of two parts, the lower forming a plinth for the upper part, which is cone-shaped. The best type is the 'Easy Pack' which is 7 in (17·5 cm) deep and 2 in (5 cm) across the top. Actually, this brand is made of aluminium and enamelled green, and is obtainable from Joseph Bentley, Barrow-on-Humber. There are also plastic ones which, I hope, will never replace the old favourites.

Arranging

I have deliberately avoided giving more than the general outline of cultivation required for show sweet peas because I know that most seed suppliers give very helpful advice and offer their own informative books about it. However, while a large number of growers can grow magnificent heads of flowers, they simply fail to show them properly. Furthermore, although they know (by watching others) how to stage them, they find it difficult to arrange their blooms properly. Nothing irritates more than when you see your competitor's exhibits all blossoms, eyes front, in soldierlike formation, while yours look tattered and weary through being handled too much. The more you handle sweet peas the worse they look, so you should stage them in the most methodical way that you possibly can, involving the minimum of handling.

The vases in which you stand your blooms are 2 in (5 cm) in diameter. They will hold either twelve stems, nine, six, or whatever the case may be, so that the heads form a half-opened fan. For the lesser numbers they can make a flat quarter circle. If a dozen, there should be three ranks – at the back you put five, in front of them four, and most forward, the remaining three. When they have all been positioned you will have up to fifty blossoms, all hardly touching, the topmost being around a foot (30 cm) above the rim of the vase. To insert them in that vase is the problem.

The small cone-like vase has to be packed with something into which the sweet pea stems can be inserted. There is nothing better than the stems of common rushes (*Juncus glaucus*) which grow wild in country ditches and marshes; they are pithy and grooved and when packed tightly they grip the sweet pea stems like a clamp. Failing that, there are other kinds of rushes growing in various damp places, or one must search for the nearest substitutes that are available.

When you get your rushes, you clasp a handful about 2 in (5 cm) across, cut the tops and bottoms level, then invert and push the thinnest ends into the vase as far as you can. Having done that so that they are tightly packed, you then cut off the protruding portions, leaving a quarter of an inch (6 mm) above the rim of the vase. This operation is best done with a very fine saw or a bread knife, rather than secateurs. You then hold the vase upside down and bang it on the table to drive the rushes in a bit further. Now you have a flat top. With a gloved thumb press down the rushes in the middle so that they go to the bottom of the cone, leaving a slight depression at the top. You then put in a little water if the rushes are dry, but leave the topping up until the job is finished.

The sweet peas look better if there is a ruff of foliage hiding the tops of the rushes and the rim of the vase. This should consist of two sections of sweet pea leaves, each with a pair of lobes. The first piece is inserted at the middle of the back of the exhibit. The thickish stem is sharpened with a knife to make it possible to push it down in between the vase and the rushes, which can be done with the help of a pointed wooden meat skewer, or something similar. That done, you insert five stems into the rushes at the back as close to the leaves as possible, the outer ones sloping outwards to the extent of the angle of the vase side. By using the skewer you are able to insert the blooms to the required height. Next, put in four stems across the middle so that they do not hide the flowers behind, positioning them between the rear flowers as it were, but more upright. That done, fix the front row of three in line with the middle ones of the back row. Finally, squeeze the skewer down the centre of the front to make a hole for the piece of leafage which is to form the front part of the ruff. Top up with water.

When selecting the blooms, you should remember that what the judges look for are true shadings throughout the stems of one variety. They also look for shape and perfect form of the individual flowers, which should be spaced as equally apart as is possible up the stem, and they like strong stems with plenty of 'timber'. It is better to have all the stems with four flowers apiece rather than, say, one or two fives, with threes to make up the number. You cannot do much dressing of blooms, but there have been instances where I have used a very fine pair of scissors to trim off carefully some discoloured edges that have been noticeable.

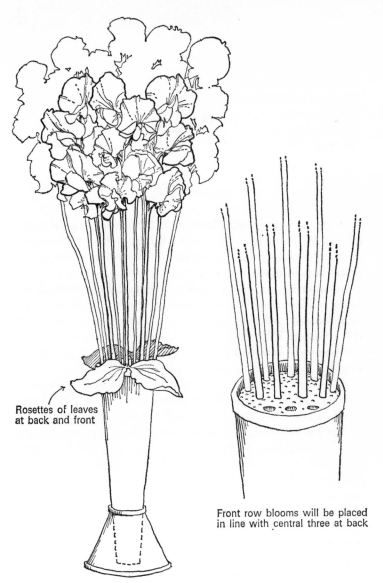

Rosettes of leaves
at back and front

Front row blooms will be placed
in line with central three at back

12. *Arranging sweet peas in rush stems*

14

Roses

Although late June is the best time of year for roses there are classes for them in most August flower shows, therefore if one becomes a devoted enthusiast, it is possible to be in the prizes lists in both seasons. At the August shows, in which I am primarily interested, there are often classes for four or six large blooms, a separate specimen bloom, and three stems of floribundas. Assuming that you know and do cultivate these flowers like everyone else who grows them well, these notes are not intended to do more than assist you in making the best of what you grow.

Roses can be a source of great disappointment. The keen amateur gets them to a state of perfection, proudly places them in the allotted position, and views those of his rivals with a certain feeling of satisfaction, quite sure that his own are the best. Alas, a few hours later, when the judges have gone, they are not even in the first three, while those others that were only half open when staged have not only developed but also been given the awards. The problem is to have the blooms at the state of perfection at that hour when they are under scrutiny, for the great fault with this glorious flower is that it is at its best for a very brief hour or two after opening.

The experts carry out all sorts of extraordinary practices to beat their rivals. They tie, clip, dress and shade their blooms, spending hours in doing so, and are quite prepared to spoil several flowers in the process. Personally I don't think all the effort made is compatible with the results, unless one is very anxious to excel as a summer exhibitor.

About three days before a show, the exhibitors look for the buds that are just showing colour. They tie them with soft wool around their middles just inside the lower row of petals, and then release them gradually in the course of the next two days. This causes the rest of the petals to grow longer. Shade cones are then put over the selected heads, and the blooms are cut on the evening of the day before the show. The petals are then smoothed out with the fingers, or brushed with a camel-hair brush, any blemished edges being carefully trimmed off with scissors. After this they are tied up again and taken to the show, where they are placed in suitable vases, the last task being finally to remove the strands of wool just before judging is due to start. The whole procedure is described in detail in specialists' books on the growing of roses.

For the August shows particularly, you can win without going to all that trouble. During one part of my career I used to compete in a district show where there were several large gardens, similar to the one under my care, and rivalry was keen but friendly. Among our colleagues was an aged man who boasted that he could not be beaten with regard to roses. Actually, this was only because we other gardeners refrained from competing, as an act of kindness. But one particular year the old man begged me to enter in order to keep the classes in the schedule, for his own flowers were a failure and he would not be entering any. This was a fortnight before the event. I had some good beds of roses in an orchard, grown especially for cutting, so I brought them up to show conditions quickly. I watered them thoroughly. Next day I sprinkled saltpetre thinly over the loamy soil, shallowly hoed it in, and then watered again. A week before the show I looked for the stems which had bunches of buds at their tops, and pinched out all except the best one on each.

I left them alone until the day of the show, getting up at dawn to cut those that were about three parts open. I removed the lower foliage of the long-as-possible stems and rubbed off the thorns of the bottom half, placing the ends in containers with a few inches of water inside. They were taken to the show like that. There, the proper vases were prepared by putting in a little curled-up wire-netting and half filling with water. Once the blooms were positioned, more water was added. Surprisingly, there were more entries than usual in those classes, this being due to the old man having appealed not only to me, but to others as well. My roses won the first prize because they were at their peak at judging time, and also that fillip of saltpetre had given them additional vigour and colour.

Selection

Although it is inadvisable to grow roses for exhibition without going into the business thoroughly, one can have the idea of doing so in mind when selecting the varieties for planting in the garden. As with many florists' flowers, there are hundreds of new varieties coming along, the number of successful ones being very small indeed. However, by studying several catalogues and also the selection tables of the Royal National Rose Society, it is possible to have a small collection that will not only give you first-class flowers in June, for the local show on the rectory lawn, but also provide you with prize-winners during August. They must be sizeable, of good shape, and keep clean in spite of weather.

At the time of writing this book, the six varieties I most favour are 'Alec's Red', 'Chicago Peace', 'McGredy's Yellow', 'Stella', 'Super Star' and 'Wendy Cussons'. They cover a fine range of colours, and descriptions are available in many catalogues.

There are differences of opinion among the experts about the best rootstocks. So much depends upon soil, weather, and district in deciding which is the best, and you strike lucky if you have the right ones for your own situation and conditions. Even if you study rose cultivation thoroughly you still experience hazards you cannot account for.

Pruning

One of the most important tasks is pruning the bushes and there are many opinions about the best time to do it. One expert will advise the middle of February, and another will contend that late March is better. Much depends upon the soil and the situation. However, I am inclined to February pruning. Also, having grown roses on all sorts of soil, I find it dangerous to prune drastically on light sandy, gravelly, peaty, or chalky soils. Only on heavy soils can it be done severely, and then only when the rose bushes have very strong rootstocks.

Pests and Diseases

The chief problems in the way of parasites that must never be left to chance are greenfly, all sorts of sawfly (leafcurl caused by these), thrips and maggots. Then there is the black spot that is most prevalent in healthy airs, but a more insidious bother is powdery mildew. There are constant new sorts of systemic insecticides and fungicides being formulated to counter these things, and one should be aware of them and of the necessity for using them. A really authoritative book is essential, but so is an eagerness to study all fresh literature issued by the Royal National Rose Society and by the manufacturers of remedies, such as ICI, Murphy, PBI and others.

Showing

Among the professionals there is a jargon which indicates in the fewest possible words certain aspects of growing roses for showing. One is 'confused centre' which means the middle of the flower is of bad form. 'De-shooting' means cutting out the softest shoots of a bush to allow more room for the rest. 'Over-blown' means the flowers have opened too far to appeal to the judges. An 'over-dressed' bloom is one that has received too much attention from the grower who coaxes the petals back with his fingers, or a brush. Where there is a bad petal at the back it may be useful to pluck it off if the spot can be partially hidden by the other petals behind it. It is bad to pull them away to the extent that there is an obvious gap.

Wire supports can be given to individual blooms, particularly at special rose shows, but are inadvisable for just one or two classes in the general August events. Most of the judges at specialist shows have standards different from those who have to adjudicate in a general way. Whereas the specialists will tolerate supports, the others may consider such things as being detrimental.

In case you want to use them, there are somewhat expensive tinned rose wires of heavy gauge, or you can obtain what the florists know as blue stub wires, in varying gauges, the thicker ones being most suitable. You also need a little binding, or bouquet wire sold by the reel. A chat with a friendly florist will do much to make you familiar with what is available. In fact, you may receive a lesson on the two different methods of fixing the wires. The usual way is to insert one end of the stiff wire into the seed pod of the flower and then bind it to the stem lower down. The better method is to make a small ring at the end of one of the wires, just large enough to hold the seed pod, and then bind lower down the stem as in the other method.

Roses do not seem to have air bubble bothers like many flowers, therefore it is better, in view of the thorns, to cut the stems with sharp secateurs. When placing them in their final show vases, if the foliage is clean and healthy it is best to leave the top leaves intact, removing only those below the water line; then arrange the blossoms so that each flower is seen distinctly from the front, the heads being as stiff and upright as possible. The longer the stems, the more they stand up above those in the other vases and, as already mentioned, a little wire-netting inside the vase will keep them in position; also if the lower thorns are either snipped or snapped off, the stems go in quite well. Once positioned, remember to top up the vase with water, taking care not to spill any on the table – that always detracts. Remember that any suggestion of a bud on hybrid tea roses will cause instant disqualification.

Floribundas

In the case of floribundas, it is freshness and fulsomeness that makes the best impression. The judges are influenced by the number of clean blossoms on a spray; if there are one or two faded blossoms they should be slithered off at the base of the stalks. If the class is for three or more sprays, whether or not to include different varieties depends upon availability. If single sprays of 'Evelyn Fison' or 'Queen Elizabeth' or 'Vesper' are equal in quality, I would rather use those than three of just one variety – but I would not include two of one and a single spray of another. In short, either use three of one variety, or three single blooms of separate sorts when that is the stipulated number.

To end these brief notes about the rose, I recount two true experiences – both with a moral if you like. At one show was a gardener trying to impress his rivals at the outset by the grand blooms he was staging against them. He patronisingly offered the half-open blooms he had brought along as spares to anyone who cared to have them. One bright adversary, whose ethics were open to question, accepted; deciding they were more promising, he removed his own entry, exchanging them for these discarded flowers. He got the first prize, but the man to whom they really belonged was unplaced – it was a hot day and all the other roses opened too quickly.

The other occasion was when I was asked to judge at a village rose and sweet pea show which had been organised by a man who regarded himself as an authority on all such matters. Before I began, he gave me a lecture to the effect that I had got to be strict and, if any rules were broken, be sure to disqualify. In every rose class for a set number of blooms I found an entry in which unopened buds had not been removed. As these could have developed into flowers I disqualified them. They were not his, but they belonged to his wife! Whether he was pleased or not I never found out – he never spoke to me again.

15

Gladioli

Some gardeners grow gladioli merely to decorate the flower borders, but they are seldom very satisfactory. They soon become messy and only daily attention will keep them presentable. Many more gardeners grow them just for cutting, which is a better proposition as they produce their spikes over a fairly long period – but they ought to be grown in the kitchen garden because the cutting has to be done before the florets open or they quickly perish. I have often grown them purely for competition, selling the unwanted ones to the local florist to help cover the cost of new corms.

These flowers, especially the giant varieties, make such an impression upon the public, and more so the judges, that they are most frequently awarded the blue ribbon for the best exhibit in the whole of the village show. In order to win you must grow them well, but they are among the least difficult of show flowers to cultivate if you take a common-sense attitude.

One of the first problems is to have enough blooms on the day they are wanted. This is only partially solved by planting the corms at calculated times. You must take into consideration whether varieties are early or late, and where you live, for it is obvious that the south is a warmer place than the north. Then there is the hazard of the weather which you can only allow for by planting an assortment of varieties.

In my district, the south, I assume that all being well the early flowering ones will start to bloom just three calendar months from planting; the mid-season will take around fifteen weeks, while the lates need a fortnight longer. Therefore, if I have a limited number of corms, I would plant all the early, the mid-season and the late together, about fifteen weeks before the show date. Should the season be warm the lates will arrive at the right time, or if it is cool the earlies may serve my purpose. If the season is normal there may be plenty of all of them.

For competitive purposes, unless the smaller types such as the 'Butterfly', 'Primulinus', or 'Miniatures' are stipulated, it is always best to concentrate upon the large-flowered varieties. They need not be the expensive ones; in fact, like the rest of the flowers we grow for showing, the ones that have stood the test of time are most likely to win. Apart from usually being superior to the majority of novelties, their names are familiar to the judges who do not like their knowledge being questioned.

Varieties

There are comparatively few exclusive gladioli specialists such as you find among rosarians, but quite a lot of firms offer corms of the better varieties. If I were growing only six dozen plants say, and one cannot very well have fewer to obtain any degree of success, for earlies I would have 'Flower Song' which produces a spike of twenty buds, with about eight flowers open at once. The colour is butter yellow. A second early choice would be 'Maria Goretti', a pure white wonder. In the mid-season category, I would have 'Spic and Span' (of a salmon colour) and 'Bloemfontein' (more apricot than salmon). 'Pink Sensation' makes an exceptionally wonderful late spike, while I am still fond of the glorious pink 'Picardy' with which I used to win many awards.

Of course, there are others equally as good, or better than

these, catalogues being good guides. However, if a start was made with that selection, after one season the best could be retained while others replaced the ones regarded as not so good. If that selection was planted during the first week of May it would be surprising if there were not enough good spikes on 15th August to give a single vase class at least.

Cultivation

Cultivation is much the same as for show vegetables. The roots should not touch manure, therefore it should be put in the lower spit. Drainage is more important. Leafmould and sedge peat forked into the top will be most helpful. At planting time I like to work in a little tomato or rose fertiliser. If the soil is acid a slight dust of lime is advisable. Fish meal is helpful during the growing season. Some growers apply dried blood – it contains everything and gives the flowers colour.

The corms need spacing 6 in (15 cm) apart in rows that are spaced 9 in (22·5 cm) apart, making a bed of four rows, and then a gangway of 18 in (45 cm) if a quantity is being grown. Do not plant too deeply, a depth of 4 in (10 cm) being ample.

If you buy corms, on inspection or by catalogue, the sizes are important. Those stated to be 1 in (2·5 cm) are best. They should always be the shape of seedling onions, with high crowns and bulging bottoms, rather than shallow like the majority of onions that are grown from 'sets'. Considerable expense is saved by growing one's own corms from 'spawn'. This consists of the clusters of cormlets that hang around the parent corm when you lift in autumn. Having saved them through winter, you sow in spring, very similarly to the way you grow peas. Carefully sorted out at the end of the summer, the best are then planted fairly closely together the year after that, so taking three seasons to get them to maturity. The shortest period in which I've obtained blooms from cormlets was one year. The variety was 'Picardy', and the light sandy soil plus a warm summer combined to bring this about.

Diseases

Unfortunately, gladioli, right from the corm state, are prone to all sorts of diseases that have to be guarded against. Those of a fungoid nature are generally transmitted by the corms and to counter these troubles, the corms are dipped in a solution of captan or Benlate before planting. The instructions for use need to be studied. If, in spite of this treatment, the leaves of any plants turn yellow prematurely, they will probably be affected by dry rot and should be carefully lifted and burned. There is another disease, fusarium yellows, producing much the same effect, and the cure is the same. An examination of the corms will reveal that they have turned blackish brown and unless completely cleared will pass the disease to the rest. However, by taking the precaution of dipping and always obtaining clean stock, these troubles can generally be avoided. Botrytis is present when the blooms, stems and leaves develop brown spots, and these mostly appear in a wet season. Benlate should clear the trouble, or be a preventative.

The worst enemy, in the south of England, is gladioli thrip – this pest is of comparative recent introduction. The insect spends only the winter season inside the corm, therefore if the plants are sprayed frequently, before the thrip can get down to the corms, this is the best way to prevent them becoming established. BHC, derris or malathion sprayed every two or three weeks from the time the leaves are about 6 in (15 cm) high, will ensure that.

Supports

These grand exhibition varieties should be given supports directly the spikes begin to form buds. Best for this purpose are 4-ft (1·2-m) bamboo canes, inserted firmly, clear of the corm. Fix the spike stem to the cane quite low down and then tie again immediately below the bottom bud. The reason for not putting in a cane earlier is that it should always be behind the criss-cross show of buds, which cannot be ascertained until they begin to form. As the spike develops, it is often advisable to carefully put a further tie towards the top. Use broad raffia rather than thin twine.

Showing

For exhibition, all the florets should face the same direction, cross-crossing evenly from the base to the top. The judges consider this very seriously. They also insist that the lowest florets are still fresh, and count the number of florets open, as well as looking for buds above with plenty of 'potential'.

In order to get the maximum number of fresh florets, some exhibitors go to all sorts of lengths to cover the ones at the base as they open, for they quickly bleach or spoil in the sun. I personally have never bothered to do this. Instead, I copy the ways of the commercial growers for supplies to florists. I cut the spike with a knife directly above the fifth leaf immediately the first floret shows a little colour. I place all the cut spikes in flower buckets almost filled with cold water and place them in the fruitroom, arranging them so that they do not touch each other, and the opening florets are not crushed at the sides of the container. A semi-light cool shed will do just as well. I start to collect these for the show about five days beforehand, and continue for three days. Most times, the best spikes are those cut on the Tuesday if the show is on the Saturday. The next problem is getting them to the venue without damage. They travel best when laid flat in long boxes, florets upwards, with soft tissue paper spaced carefully between to stop chafing. Upon arrival, take them out without delay and place the ends in water, almost up to the lower florets. After that, you position them in the vases, which need to be very heavy ones – preferably stone jars, if available. You can wedge the stems with any sort of packing, but try as you will, until you find your own technique, you will have difficulty in keeping them properly spaced, with all the florets facing you. There is nothing better than the pincushion-type of holder for keeping them in place with all faces to the front. There are various sizes available, the largest that can be accommodated by the container being best. For holding gladioli, always use containers with very large bases.

When selecting the spikes it is best to not use those whose lower florets are fading. Fewer open florets with plenty of unopened ones are more promising. If you are desperate and have to use such, it is best to cut off the faded ones. Bent stems are drawbacks, and it is considered to be a fault if the criss-crossed florets are spaced so far apart that the stem can be seen between them. If you do manage to select, in perfect condition, whatever number of spikes is asked for, they will look simply gorgeous – it should not be difficult.

16

Pot Plants

In our local flower show schedule are no less than eight classes for various pot plants. Geraniums, fuchsias, gloxinias and coleus are specified, the other classes being for either any kind with flowers or for foliage alone. In some other shows you will find special classes for begonias, saintpaulias (African violets), or whatever appeals to members of the local committee.

There are often special rules and regulations, such as a limit to the size of the pot, and a stipulation that the entrant must have owned the plant for so long, in case some prankster visits the nearest florist just before the show and exhibits a bought plant purported to be of his or her own growing.

To go into all the details of cultivation regarding these flowers is impracticable, but I hope that the few hints I can give are helpful.

Where the class is open to any flowering plant, usually the gloxinias and begonias are favoured by the judges. Fuchsias come a bad third. There are entrants who try to be clever and different, staging such plants as achimenes or shrimp plants. This causes arguments, for achimenes comprise several tubers, and in the case of shrimp plants there will often be more than one in the same pot. While the judges do not disqualify them, they most often pass them by. Therefore, if you have anything that is definitely a single plant and nothing else, put that in the show, rather than a composite.

Undoubtedly, the tuberous begonias with their large bright flowers, when grown well make all other flowering pot plants look comparatively dull. You can buy the dry tubers of these and start them into growth in a warm greenhouse during March. The usual procedure is to place them in damp leaf-mould or sedge peat until they send out rootlets and top growth and then plant them in suitably sized pots. A good soil mixture is four parts loam, four parts leafmould or sedge peat, two parts sand, two parts dried cow manure, and a little broken charcoal. I find it less bothersome to obtain instead ready-mixed John Innes No. 1 Potting Compost, and for begonias, gloxinias and saintpaulias, add more leafmould or sedge peat to make the texture soft. It should drain easily yet retain water for some time.

Shade the plants from bright sunshine, keep soil constantly moist, spray daily with clear water. Give a little liquid fertiliser when the plants are growing nicely. Look out for pests and spray if any are suspected, a nicotine emulsion being one of the safest, for the foliage is tender and apt to be scorched, especially if not shaded.

Gloxinias, although not so brilliant, can, when well grown, be more attractive than begonias. The best position is where there is full warmth through glass but also some shade between glass and plant, such as pieces of gauze or curtaining. Good plants will produce up a to a dozen lovely flowers at one time.

Saintpaulias belong to the same family as the gloxinias, and love much the same conditions. The most successful grower I've met, apart from the commercial specialists, was a lady who had a row of them on a ledge between the window and the kitchen sink. The occasional steam from the washing-up seemed to suit their needs perfectly.

Fuchsias when entered against begonias and gloxinias, they only succeed when the latter are much inferior. Their season has passed in August, whereas it is the ideal month for the brighter plants. However, if you grow fuchsias, either as bushes or as standards, they are worth entering wherever possible on the off-chance that the judges prefer those, especially when the specimens of the more flamboyant plants are weak.

Geraniums must be exceptionally grand to beat the gloxinias, begonias, and so on, in a class which is a free-for-all. Notwithstanding, if I had a glorious plant that was stronger than my gloxinias or begonias, I would enter it instead. It depends upon its splendour and the amount of fresh flowers on view. A modest plant stands a better chance in a class confined to the genus than it does among other kinds.

Very often there is a class *for any other pot plant*, which means that those listed in the special classes are barred. In that case it is best to go for any startling subject you may happen to have. Only last season I obtained the first prize for an aechmea, or urn plant, which was in fine form at the time. Other plants that make an impact are hippeastrums, anthuriums, caladiums, and blacking plants (*Hibiscus rosa-sinensis*). These come before subjects like browallias, exacums, busy lizzies, (impatiens) and suchlike annuals, or perennials, easily raised from seed. A well-grown *Begonia rex* will beat the lot.

In the opening paragraph of this chapter I mentioned that there was a class for coleus. This is entirely a foliage plant, but if entered in a class where any type of foliage specimen is eligible, it stands little chance of beating many other kinds, like the caladiums, philodendrons, the best of the ferns, peperomias and rex begonias. Nevertheless, if I had an outstanding specimen for colour and cleanliness, I might prefer it to anything else in the greenhouse.

So far, only those plants likely to be in condition for the

August shows have been mentioned. There are others more suitable for competition at the spring bulb shows, although there are invitations to show them in the height of summer as an additional attraction to the roses and sweet peas.

For spring we can grow azaleas, calceolarias, cinerarias, cyclamen, primulas, schizanthuses and stocks. An azalea grown in a small pot, just on the verge of opening all its blossoms, is irresistible. Quite apart from that, cyclamen when well grown undoubtedly make a deep impression upon the judges. Whether such plants are successful or not, very much depends upon the vigour and quality of the others.

In many shows there are classes for collections of cacti and/or succulent plants, and I've often been asked to judge these without really knowing much about the 'flowers of the desert'. There are many other judges of similar standing. It is most likely that the competitors know more about them than we who have to decide.

Most times, by hearing comments from others, and keeping my own counsel, I am influenced by the general appearance, including the size and condition of the container, which should be in keeping with its occupant. The plant itself should, if possible, be bearing flowers and look thoroughly happy. Any apparent deformities or uninteresting features are weighed against the virtues and a decision made accordingly.

Showing

Whatever we grow, wherever we show, it can be assumed that the judges will be considerably influenced by the pots our plants are living in, especially whether they are clean or otherwise, for they should enhance rather than detract from the general appearance.

Pots should be on the small side, in proportion to the overall spread of the plants. Where plants need supports these should be as unobtrusive as possible. In short, the plants and the containers should appear exuberant. If there are any diseased or injured leaves, it is better to remove them even if this incurs unfavourable criticism, for it is the lesser of the faults.

Should you have two plants that seem equally good and are undecided which to enter, the one that demands most skill in producing is preferable. Actually, when in that predicament, if possible I take both along to the show, and having compared them with those of my rivals, I make the final decision at the last minute. When one sees another entry that is decidedly superior to that cyclamen, say, then put in the grand cineraria instead, although, by all accounts, it is not regarded as being equal in quality. If you stage the cyclamen which is inferior to the others you may get nothing, but if your cineraria is a good plant it can win a second place, so gaining points for that cup.

17

Miscellaneous Flowers

DELPHINIUMS

Although these majestic flowers make most impressive vases in competitions, when shows are confined to them alone, they are not worth cultivating specifically for local events. Their season is wrong, and they are individualistic, by which I mean that they do not fit in with other herbaceous flowers in collections, either dwarfing them or lacking in harmonising foliage.

Notwithstanding, I have at times had ideas enough to sow seed of Pacific Hybrids, in early spring, with a view to getting enough spikes to fill a vase in a collection. Only once did I do so and was not awarded the top prize, these delphiniums being my downfall. They looked grand enough, but the judges had memories of those enormous spikes of varieties like 'Blue Nile' and 'Icecap'. Most years the seed-lings, or the late spikes of the old plants, are infested with mildew.

Another problem with delphiniums is air bubbles. The best way to avoid them is to cut the stems very low down in the first instance, using a knife and slicing through at an angle. Then remove the lower leaves, and make an upward cleavage of the stem for an inch or so before putting it in water as near as possible to the lower florets. When you stage at the show, hold the stem end under water in the bucket while cutting it through to the proper length so that the spike of colour begins a mere few inches clear of the vase. This is for individual classes, and not when these flowers are included in collections of perennials. Then you allow more stem and hope for the best.

PANSIES

Nowadays, there are often classes for twelve heads of pansies. Sometimes a number of colours are stipulated, but usually the schedule gives only the number of blooms. These are best staged on a board, the blooms being laid flat upon its top in a straightforward alignment of three rows of four each. They will quickly perish unless the short stems behind the faces are inserted in water. A 'board' can be made by finding a tailor's cardboard suit box, which can be cut down to size if there is a restriction – if not, keep it intact. Measure the lid to ascertain where the middle of each flower will be, and puncture holes about $\frac{1}{2}$ in (12 mm) in diameter accordingly. Then place the lid on the lower part, and by inserting a pencil make a dot on the base of the box; you then glue over each spot a small container, such as a chemist's measuring cup or a paste jar, and then replace the lid. Over the lid you fasten, by tucking underneath and gluing, a double thickness of white paper. You then pierce this through where the holes are; now carefully put some water into the containers, never overfilling or disaster will follow. You then carefully insert the stalks, that should be just long enough to reach the bottom of the containers, but not allowing the blooms to 'ride'.

You can grow pansies especially for show by sowing, in early spring indoors, seed of a noted strain – such as the 'Roggli' – if the show is in August. If earlier in summer, as an addition to roses and sweet peas, autumn sowing is best.

Pansies are moisture-loving, enjoying rich ground and leaf-mould. If you want them for a certain day, pick off all buds until a week before the show, gathering the selected flowers during the two days preceding the show, putting their longish stems in water until the time of taking them to the show. When you arrive, lay them out of the bench and decide where each will go before placing on the board in the final position. The judges look for size and shapeliness, roundness being a desirable quality.

Violas need much the same sort of treatment. While there are differences in the various sorts of violas and pansies, causing a certain degree of 'punditry' among the experts, in some instances there is such a similarity that only they can differentiate.

IRISES

By growing the many species and varieties it is possible, without much difficulty, to have irises on view every day of the year. However, they seldom make much impact at general flower shows, the chief competitions being held for the German or flag varieties during early June, or for the dwarf bulbous kinds in early spring as sidelines to the alpines and the daffodils. There is an Iris Society, with very enthusiastic members comprising private individuals and 'the trade'. It seems to me that it's mainly a matter of getting the newest expensive varieties in order to stage the winning entries in the various classes held, most often in the RHS Hall in London. If you have the right sort of soil and a sunny garden, and are prepared to join the enthusiasts, you will be much welcomed and will quite soon become an authority.

There is a story about an iris fanatic who confined his cultivations to the accepted aristocrats of the genus. His favourite aunt always came to stay at Christmas, Easter and August Bank Holiday. On each occasion he took her round the garden until she made the comment 'You have a wonderful garden, I must say, Cuthbert, but you never have any flowers.'

I have yet to see irises excel in general shows.

PEONIES

Precisely the same comments can be made about peonies as about irises, except that their season is very limited. Unless you are content, apart from being a specialist, to show only in early summer, the space they would take up in the garden can be better used.

AURICULAS

These members of the primrose family fascinate me, and seeing that they take up comparatively little space, they should appeal very much to the competitive spirit. However, their cultivation needs considerable knowledge and understanding, and opportunities for showing them are so few that I do not advise growing them unless one gets the bug for doing so; therefore the inclusion of any hints about their cultivation in this book is not necessary.

CARNATIONS

The carnation genus consists of several distinct types. First are the malmaisons that demand special greenhouse treatment. They have virtually faded away, along with the passing of large estate gardens. Next are the tree or perpetual varieties raised by the acre under glass for the florist trade. Then come the border carnations, including variations of them such as the picotees. These, much like irises and the other flowers mentioned in this chapter, are the pride of experts rather than the general gardener, and if one takes up their cultivation, many of the general crops must be forfeited in order to give these the necessary attention. Their season is summer, when the rose and sweet pea shows are being held and there could be classes for them, but not often.

Although they are very perennial, the people who grow for showing keep their plants for only one season and then, having taken layered shoots off them, discard the parent plants. Actually the plants bear more prolifically in the second season, especially if the soil is light, rich, well-drained and of a calcareous nature.

It is rather a costly business, obtaining the latest varieties of show standard, and there are pest troubles such as wireworms, greenfly and rusts. The stems have to be supported and there has to be disbudding in order to have large outstanding blooms. Once you have your blooms they are quite easy to stage, but weak stems are apt to flop. These are definitely specialists' flowers.

NARCISSUS

During the week that this section was written we had a gardening meeting, and as it was the daffodil season there was a competition for six heads of these most common of spring flowers. There were about twenty entries and I obtained the top prize although, in my estimation, there were others that could have been placed before mine – if they had been staged properly. They were more modern varieties than my six blooms of 'Rembrandt'. I chose the right vase, a wine-tinted glass shaped like an inverted cornet with a flat inconspicuous base. I gathered some privet shoots, rubbed off the leaves, and packed them in the vase quite close together, leaving just enough spaces to insert the bases of the daffodil stems about two inches into the water.

The daffodils were gathered the day before, selecting those just on the point of fully opening; I put them in cans of water almost to their necks, and stood them in a cool room. At the meeting, I simply took my vase with the privet already in position, and half filled it with water; I laid my daffodils flat on the table and decided which I would use, leaving the best one for the front position. Their ends were slightly shortened, and when inserted the stems stood up straight and strong, the back row canting away from the viewers, so setting off their trumpets; I adjusted them up or down in the privet to give the desired height, forming a frontal bouquet. A few leaves were also inserted among them where there was a gap. The vase was topped up with water and, having scanned the efforts of my rivals, I concluded that I would get first or nothing, depending upon the impact the blooms made on the judge. Chatting afterwards, I asked him why some of the others were not given preference. He pointed out their weakness, such as stems too short, damage to the petals and so on. He could not fault mine except for variety, but even then it was still good, with the nice flat and even corolla, and the neat clean trumpet to form a perfect balance.

There is little more to add to this, whether it be for the highly coloured narcissus varieties in other classes, or a class of mixtures. You simply buy the bulbs and grow them in good soil. If you grow several varieties to spread over a season, you will then have one of them, at least, in prime condition on the day.

ARUMS

At one period when in charge of some large gardens where we sold our surplus, I was barred from showing in the gardening classes but could compete against a lot of keen nurseries producing flowers for market. Several firms grew arum lilies and so there was a class for half a dozen blooms of this lovely florist's flower mainly used in emblems. I had a good strain and decided to enter, but was not sure whether to stage fully open blooms or those three parts open, the white sheath just unfolding from around the golden spadix. I took along two half dozens. Upon arrival, I was taken aback at seeing about a dozen competitors all showing fully open blossoms. They all looked magnificently alike. Mine were no better so, in desperation, I staged the ones partially open. They won the award. At the next annual show in that identical class all the competitors staged them three parts open. I decided to do the opposite, and again was proved the winner. My rivals did not complain to me, but what they had to say about the judges was nobody's business! Actually they were different people. On each occasion these judges had to make decisions amongst blooms that all seemed equal and therefore chose those that *looked* different. It was my awareness, rather than any superior skill, that brought the rewards.

There are still many other flowers that I have made no comments on, but I hope that I have given enough hints to cover them all, and to reveal to the aspiring exhibitor that apart from the skill of growing things there is an art in showing them to the best advantage. It is no use grumbling about the judges being inefficient; one must be ever alert and be not only conversant with stereotyped practices, but be able to decide when to comply with them or be experimental. Never mind if you find anyone cheating – it only creates bad feeling against you if you complain. If you stage the best you can muster, in the most 'showable' way, you will more often than not be among the top prizewinners and, furthermore, gain the utmost respect from your true rivals.

18

Apples and Pears

Although there are in almost all local August flower shows classes for fruit, they are most times badly supported and the quality is poor. If anyone is thinking about becoming a specialist in some line of gardening, but is still undecided as to which to choose, I wholeheartedly suggest it be the cultivation of tree fruits. This is a department that has so much to commend it. Unlike greenhouse crops, or flowers of many kinds, you can apply your skill when you feel like it instead of being a slave to continuous attentions.

Successful growing of crops of a national competitive standard does depend very much upon where you live, though there are experts living in all parts of the country who *do* excel. Whether or not you can achieve such excellence, you can, at least, acquire a local reputation within a few years.

The requisite initial knowledge can be obtained from reliable books (see Garden Literature, p. 163). You can also learn all about the most modern methods of controlling pests by studying literature obtainable from firms like Murphy, ICI, PBI, and such sundries men as Joseph Bentley, Barrow-on-Humber. Fruit tree catalogues are getting smaller and scarcer, but there are still some good ones issued by firms including John Scott and Co, Marriott, Somerset, and Rivers and Son, Sawbridgeworth, Herts. By these various means of gaining knowledge, one can become familiar with the methods of obtaining first-class fruit crops. Some of the hints I now give may, or may not, be included in those other sources of information. My notes are intended to be either supplementary or complementary to them.

APPLES

As you know, there are distinct dessert apples and those that are purely culinary. There are also a few varieties considered to be suitable for both classes. Among the latter are Belle de Boskoop, Blenheim Orange, Gasgoyne's Scarlet, and Herring's Pippin. I have grown all four varieties, but only shown one of them in both classes, it so happening that I had some very nice medium-sized Blenheims, and also some whoppers that were large enough to cook. I have shown Gasgoyne's Scarlet as a dessert, purely for colour, it not being fancied by many judges on account of its poor flavour. Herring's Pippin is a much better proposition; Belle de Boskoop is thought highly of, but it lacks the colour of Herring's Pippin, therefore if one is selecting for showing, Blenheim and Herring's are preferred. Blenheim takes a long time to achieve bearing propensities, and therefore should be regarded as a wonderful long-term investment rather than as an early possibility.

Dessert Varieties

Almost always the winner at the local August show is Beauty of Bath; although small it predominates on account of its colour. But there are other more reliable and superior varieties than can appeal to discerning judges. George Cave, Laxton's Epicure and Scarlet Pimpernel are excellent. For putting up early collections I would plant the lot. If only one, it must be George Cave.

In September, we have Ellison's Orange, James Grieve, Fortune, and Tydeman's Early Worcester. Some of the August apples will also last into September, just as the September varieties will often last into October, when Lord Lambourne, Charles Ross, Egremont Russet, Sunset and Herring's Pippin are also available.

Other good show varieties that are available in October or November are the famous Cox's Orange Pippin, which is when grown perfectly the supreme apple, Ribston Pippin, an excellent show fruit, and Laxton's Superb, much easier than the other two. Cox's seem to flourish best in warm counties where the soil is somewhat stiffish. It needs constant spraying and is rather choosy about where it will grow well. Ribston also loves warmth, although is less fussy about conditions.

In my opinion, if you can grow as many as possible of those dessert varieties I have mentioned, not only will you have a fine selection, but they will all help each other as regards pollination. There should not be a barren tree among them.

Culinary Varieties

Whereas dessert fruits should be of medium size, and colour is all important, the culinary varieties need to be as bulky as possible, taking into regard the condition and quality. They need not be ripe, nor in season; therefore if you grow varieties that will attain size rapidly and also, if for late shows, remain in good condition, there is little else to consider in this respect.

My selection in order of growing to mature size rather than for any other qualities is:

Arthur Turner	Howgate Wonder
Bramley's Seedling	Lord Derby
George Neal	Rev W. Wilks

There are a few others which are quite good for early

showing, such as Warner's King, but they seldom keep in perfect condition for any length of time. I think this half dozen is ample for normal purposes.

The 'cookers' listed and your favourite dozen dessert varieties that will grow satisfactorily in the prevailing conditions comprise an orchard assortment that should suit every enthusiast – at least, as an initial interest in these fruits.

Rootstocks

You will read in all books on the subject that small bush trees grown on rootstock Malling IX give the quickest returns, but I prefer the stronger rootstock M26 or, if that is unavailable, MM106. I think that the fruits grown from these are superior to those that come as the dwarfest form. And if, instead of small bush trees, you have oblique cordons, they are better still.

Thinning

One of the ways to get large apples is to thin the fruitlets quite drastically, starting in early July and continuing the process for several weeks. Practically all the culinary varieties need severe thinning, whereas some of the desserts will need hardly any at all. This is particularly so with Blenheim Orange, Charles Ross, Gasgoyne's Scarlet, Herring's Pippin and Laxton's Superb. However, there are naturally small varieties that it pays to thin; observation and experience will determine which these are.

Some varieties have stubby stalks, others have long ones. In the case of the long ones, one should look for the specimen with the thickest stalk in each cluster and snip or pull it off before all others. It is unshapely? Then keep the best one of the remainder – eventually, for thinning should be spread over weeks, taking care to remove any fruits that are misshapen or blemished in any way.

I find that thinning fruit, especially after the initial once-over has been done, is best carried out while it is raining. I like to put on a raincoat and work among the trees, pulling off, rather than snipping, those that are inferior to the rest, and then applying a little fertiliser on the ground above the roots, where it will soak in. I believe in using my own fertiliser formulas for fruit, rather than relying upon a general brand. If the trees are growing strongly, phosphates and potash are the main ingredients of the mixture; if the growth is weak and fruiting is heavy, them more nitrogen is added to the other two ingredients.

Colour

With dessert varieties, colour is more vital than size, although to some extent size is also important. If you can induce the differing varieties to produce specimens that are around 3 in (7·5 cm) in diameter, all is well. Although you may find it difficult to do this, it is something to aim for when making your selections for the show. However, colour counts most. To obtain it you need sunshine and moisture and the right sort of varieties. Frequent spraying of the trees with a mistifier will help. On the dwarf trees, if you see leaves shading specimens from the sun, nip them off. If you happen to live near the seaside or in a valley where the air is moist, you are fortunate, although this last can sometimes be a drawback, for frost can be bad in such places and prevent the trees from fruiting.

Sometimes you have a number of apples full of colour, but cannot find enough of them. You can then strive to get the other fruits to the right hues by placing them on the ground under the tree several days before required. If the weather is dry and you sprinkle them with water from time to time, you can persuade them to become mellow and look more ripe than they did. They should be shielded from birds, and some slug pellets need to be sprinkled around. One gardener I knew used to get his specimens to wonderful shades by placing them in a stinging-nettle bed. Whether this kept the birds away or had a special magical effect, I never did find out.

Pruning and Spraying

As the books will tell you there are several other aspects of growing tree fruits, including pruning, of which there are many systems. You will read about the tip-bearers, like Bramley's Seedling and others. For trained trees, summer pruning is necessary; dwarf bush trees can also be summer pruned, but more judiciously. It is impossible to deal with this subject in detail in this book, which is primarily concerned with those additional attentions necessary for show work. Spraying is another aspect about which there are different ideas; some do it many times a year, some ignore it altogether – to their cost. I believe it should be done in moderation.

Bagging

Most showmen go in for 'bagging'. This means enclosing those special fruits intended for show in muslin bags while they hang on the trees, both to stop them falling to the ground and to protect them from birds and insects. These bags are shaped like those which little boys have for marbles and are fitted with similar slip strings so that they can, after being placed over the fruits, be fixed to the boughs. At one time I had several hundred of them, in varying sizes, made by one of the estate ladies. Discarded nylon stockings are really good for this purpose. Plastic is unsuitable. Butter muslin is finely perforated and allows air and sunshine to get at the fruits, which then seem to improve in finish and appearance. The bags are put on directly there are signs of damage from marauders, dealing with the fruits variety by variety – as the need arises. The bags do not lengthen the life of the fruits, which should be gathered at the normal time.

As a general rule, early dessert varieties are best left on the trees until ready to eat, therefore bags should be put over them to keep them from dropping. Mid-season varieties like Ellison's Orange and Tydeman's Early Worcester need to be gathered when you can pull them off easily, and be stored for several days before showing. James Grieve is a terror for dropping prematurely, but if bagged the apples will be safe and ready when needed. The later varieties are left on the trees as long as safely possible, the weather being the deciding factor. The culinary varieties should be left to hang, in their bags, until they simply want to drop. The size can be increased by feeding the roots with water from a perpetual drip nozzle up to the last day or two.

Early varieties can sometimes be kept much longer than their normal season by gathering them just before they are ripe, wrapping them individually in pieces of newspaper, and putting them in large biscuit tins, then piercing one or two small holes in the lids before burying the tins in the garden on the north side of a wall, covering the lid with about an inch of soil.

Staging

For transporting to the show venue the fruits should be carefully wrapped individually in newspaper and placed in a basket or hamper. On no account are the skins polished at any time. When shown they must always have that natural 'bloom' or sheen that can be removed by rubbing. Take care never to spoil this appearance – many an exhibitor has lost an award through that fault.

Apples should be put on plates, although they are most often referred to as 'dishes'. There is an art in staging them, either directly on to the plates, or completely covering the latter with white paper. I prefer strong white tissue. You also need fine woodwool, although screwed-up tissue paper can be used instead. You first of all ruffle up the woodwool and roll it into a disc; now wrap it in the tissue paper so that it will fill the pan of the plate, slightly mounded in the middle. Over this you place a sheet, or double sheet, of tissue to form a complete covering, tucking the edges under the plate. You place five of the apples evenly around the outside so that they partly rest on the ledge of the plate and partly on the sides of the mound. You next roll up more woodwool (or tissue) into a ball, and cover it with more paper and sit it in the middle of the mound, filling the space in the centre of the five apples. On that you sit the sixth apple so that it rests on the inner shoulders of the others, the ball of tissue taking the weight and also keeping the outer apples in their positions. Obviously, the inner ball will have to be shaped according to the fruits. If they are culinary varieties it will be coconut-shaped; if dessert, quite squat. Some exhibitors do not completely cover the plate but only insert the packing in the middle just to keep the fruits upright.

When selecting fruits for the dishes, the same old rule regarding evenness should be heeded. In the case of dessert varieties, I first of all look over the ones I have and pick out the one I regard as the most colourful and representative of them and place it on one side on a cloth. That will be the one in the middle of the dish when the staging is done. Then I scrutinise the rest, placing them against the selected one, and eventually by comparison manage to get the half dozen I want. It will surprise you how difficult it is to get them all alike, but remember that it is just as difficult for your rivals!

Always label the varieties, whether or not the rules call for

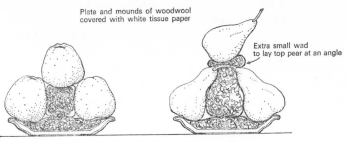

Plate and mounds of woodwool
covered with white tissue paper

Extra small wad
to lay top pear at an angle

13. *Displaying apples and pears*

you to do so. Quite often the judges at shows are not familiar
with them all, although they recognise the names. Sometimes
you are wrong and then, if there is a knowledgeable judge, he
will correct you. Never be daunted by unfortunate decisions
that do occur even in the highest circles. On one occasion I
sent some specimens to the RHS for naming and had it in
writing that they were Annie Elizabeth, a large culinary
variety. I staged them in one of their fruit shows under that
name, according to the rules, only to be told they were 'not
true to name'. I never protested on that occasion, but I did
protest once when Charles Ross was given an award for a
class of Blenheims. My complaint was upheld. We all make
mistakes.

PEARS

As with apples, one of the essentials for gaining prizes is to
have the right varieties. During August there is little choice,
but my favourite is Jargonelle – it is small but has all the right
qualities. There are some good ones in season during September and early October, among them Dr Jules Guyot,
Fondant d'Automne, Marguerite Marillat, Melton Pride and
Williams' Bon Chrétien. However, the best pears crop from
early October into the middle of November when there are

many more beautiful varieties, among them Louise Bonne of Jersey, Packham's Triumph and Emile d'Heyst.

At a national show held in late October, for a collection of six varieties, I successfully staged:

Beurré Superfin	Durondeau
Conference	Fondante de Thirriot
Doyenné du Comice	Pitmaston Duchess

In two other years, instead of one or other of the above, I put on Roosevelt and Marie Benoist. This was because rivals' specimens of the super varieties were better then than mine; my selection evidently pleased the judges.

When planting pears it is important to study pollinating abilities. For instance, I know that Jargonelle and Beurre Superfin are good companions. Conference is a wonderful pollen-producing fruit, and good for Doyenné du Comice and Beurré Hardy. Good fruit tree lists will often give an expert's opinions about this.

There may be a few other varieties worth growing for show purposes, and one or two that I have mentioned may not be regarded as classy enough from the connoisseur's point of view. Pitmaston Duchess, for example, is seldom recommended, simply because it is too large – but it's a wonderful dessert variety when in a state of near-perfection.

Grafts

Books will tell you that some varieties need to be double-grafted. Another term is 'double-worked'. The explanation is that most pears are grafted or budded on to Quince A rootstocks. Some of these varieties do not flourish when grafted directly on to such roots, and so the nurseryman first of all grafts a suitable variety on to the rootstock, and after that grafts the difficult variety on to the shortened stem of the easy one. This involves time and expense. Sometimes, to save time, the nurseryman 'splice grafts', or practises 'double shield budding'. The important thing is to remember that, of the varieties I have mentioned, those needing to be 'double worked' in one way or another are Dr Jules Guyot, Fondante de Thirriot, Jargonelle, Marguerite Marillat, Packham's Triumph and Williams' Bon Chrétien. There are other rootstocks for pears, but unfortunately they are generally inferior to the quince.

Position

Compared with apples, pears need much more warmth, good soil, moisture but drainage, and plenty of potash. They are best grown as trained trees, preferably single cordons upright on high walls. I have yet to find the right quality of fruit in the open, while fences are not as good as walls. If the trees are planted in the right position not only can attention to pruning, thinning and so forth be given comfortably, but it is a fact that fewer pest diseases are found, especially those of a fungoid nature.

Pruning, Feeding and Thinning

Pear trees are likely either to produce too many fruiting spurs and too little new wood, or to produce strong shoots every season with little fruit. These inequalities are corrected by pruning and feeding. If there are too many fruiting buds and little growth, some of them are cut away and the trees are given additional nitrogen. If the reverse, nitrogen is withheld and the pruning consists of severely shortening new growths in late summer. There are several so-called systems in this connection. The one that I have practised successfully is to cut the new shoots, when about 8 in (20 cm) long, hard back, quite close to the point from where they started. This means spreading the job over several weeks during the season. When there are too many fruiting spurs they are pruned off during the dormant period.

Thinning the fruits is of the utmost importance. This

starts earlier than for apples, the first to ripen needing attention in the middle of June. They finally need to be spaced several inches apart.

Bagging

Enclosing the fruits in muslin bags or old nylon stockings is even more necessary than for apples, for tits have a bad habit of pecking small holes in the stalk ends, into which wasps and flies can enter and completely spoil the crop.

Pests and Diseases

Most of the pests that attack apples also like pears, although sometimes not as much. Pear midge is a peculiar problem; it causes larvae to form inside the fruits, and once present it is beyond cure, except by carefully gathering all the affected fruitlets and burning them. As these midges spend a part of their lives in the soil, the latter should be disturbed as deeply as can be safely done above the roots, during the latter part of June and the whole of July. A recommended preventative is to dilute a pint of tar in two gallons of water and sprinkle this, with a fine-rosed can, all over the ground around the tree just when the blossoms are beginning to open.

Pears on walls are less likely to be attacked by black spot than are those growing in the open, especially if the position is warm and sunny, and they are thriving. As a safeguard, a fungicide containing thiram is especially good. At the same time, if the requisite amount of liquid derris is added you are disposing of several pests other than the midge. Aphids, sawfly or slugworms, weevils and so on, which lurk around most fruit trees are at least made uncomfortable.

Staging

Pears are sensitive fruits. The early ones should be gathered before they change colour. The later varieties can be left until they almost drop, for if taken early they shrivel. Put them in the cool room until they ripen. This can to some extent be gauged by gently pressing the skin close to the stalk end of each fruit. When it gives ever so slightly it is nearing ripeness. Showing aside, if you stand the fruit in a warmer room a day or two before you eat it, the flavour will then be far superior than it would be if you allowed it to ripen completely in the cool place. However, one cannot generalise about precisely what to do, for pears differ considerably. Beurré Hardy and Beurré Superfin can both feel all right on the outside but be 'sleepy' within. On the other hand, Doyenne du Comice, the most satisfying of all pears, will remain sound for a much longer time.

The chief difference between staging apples and pears is that, whereas apples are positioned stalks downwards, pears are reversed. This is purely a matter of practicability, rather than having any effect upon the fruit. The plate is prepared in precisely the same way as described for apples on p. 138 – i.e. completely covered with tissue, after placing a mound in the middle of the pan. Then a ball of woodwool, wrapped in tissue, is placed on the mound. It has to be more bulky and taller than for apples so that when the five fruits are placed around it with their stalks upwards, they are gently sloping to the middle but well apart, so that the best fruit can then be laid flat across the top to set off the collection impressively (See Fig. 13). The middle support must be prepared according to the variety. If for Pitmaston Duchess, for example, it should be narrow and columnar, or you will not get the fruits to lodge on the plate. The centre support should be level with the top ends of the stalks. In the case of Conference you need a bulkier but very tall column in order to keep the fruits well out and prevent the stalks from being broken or bruised by the best fruit when it is laid across the top. For other pears, the ball of woodwool should be moulded accordingly.

19

Stone Fruits

PLUMS

Embraced by this title are all the splendid gages, as well as those fruits we regard as plums, several of which ripen during August – just right for local flower shows. There are later ripeners, the last maturing in October, when the more limited, but interesting, fruit competitions take place.

Although plums and gages are considered to be difficult to grow in some districts, the old gardeners managed to cultivate them wherever they were, so they are always a good proposition, both as prizewinners and a utility crop.

The wonderful gages grow best against walls with east or west aspects, if the soil is carefully prepared for the roots. The trees are mostly fan-trained, and all information regarding their needs, particularly spacing and pruning, should be studied. Feeding, mulching, watering, thinning and spraying against pests are tasks that must be carried out. These are discussed again and again in books and magazines, and they are very important.

There are very important factors to be borne in mind when buying trees, for these must be of the right varieties and have the best rootstocks. Many are self-sterile, and need suitable compatible companions near them. A number of books and some catalogues contain advice about this. If one doesn't already have the necessary knowledge, one must make careful investigation.

Varieties

There are three self-fertile plums (gages) of show standard that mature in August when the shows take place. They are Denniston's Superb, Oullin's Golden Gage and the popular Victoria plums. Although they ripen approximately together, the blossoms arrive a few days apart, Denniston's being first, Victoria in mid-season and Oullin's much later. It is important to bear in mind that it is not necessarily the first to open which suffers most from frost. My experience is that Oullin's has sometimes come off worst. Together these three will ensure a selection of fruits to choose from in normal years. These varieties are also good pollinators for others that are themselves infertile, and should always be planted where there is a larger collection for spreading over the season of ripening from mid-August until the last are ready in October.

For October shows I have grown President, a very large purple culinary plum that bears flowers about the same time as Denniston's. Coe's Golden Drop, preferably planted on a warm south wall, is somewhat smallish, of a lovely amber colour, with red beauty spots, and the richest of flesh when properly ripened. Although it ripens at the end of the season it, like President, blossoms quite early and is also compatible with Denniston's.

A plum of which I am very fond is Kirke's Blue. It is of gage quality and arrives in the middle of September. The pollen of both Victoria and Oullin's helps its setting problems. A late gage is Reine Claude de Bavay, which seems to have fewer problems than the other gages and which flowers in mid-season, when it can supply pollen to Transparent Gage, as also can Victoria.

Rootstocks and Pruning

There are several forms of rootstock for plums, among them being common plum, mussel and myrobalan. If you can get trees on the recent stock, St Julian A, you should choose these in preference to any other. Some of the older stocks grow too strongly, and necessitate root pruning. Regarding top pruning, the less done the better if the trees are natural half-standards; with fan-shaped trees one should judiciously remove the strongest growths and the weakest, tying the remainder into position. I'm inclined to be more lax than rigid about this, for I find that when you train them too hard they are likely to become beset with other troubles.

Pests

One of the curses is the aphis which makes a complete mess of some varieties unless there is winter spraying with tar oil, and when you do that you increase the chances of red spider arriving in summer. It is best to study the spraying programmes of the commercial growers and adopt the most convenient. (See also under Bagging.)

Thinning

Plums have a habit of either over-bearing, or giving very sparse crops. If the trees are over-loaded, gradually (rather than all in one operation) remove unwanted fruitlets when they are about the size of hazel nuts, so that ultimately the fruits are spaced about 4 in (10 cm) apart. The trees themselves will shed many fruitlets in the heavy-cropping years but if we undertake a further thinning, this will not only vastly improve the quality of the remaining plums but will also induce more regular cropping in future years.

Bagging

Whether or not to cover the fruits with muslin bags is a matter of discretion. If the crop is limited and the choice fruits are on fan-trained trees against walls, it is definitely advisable. Wasps are sometimes a nuisance, and birds can do a lot of damage. My practice has been to keep a careful lookout for troubles, and counter them in double-quick time by doing what is necessary.

Showing

A deal of skill is needed to get those fruits from the tree to the show bench without marring their appearances, for there should be a complete covering of natural powdery 'bloom' over the blue, yellow, or white skins. The stalks should always be complete, showing the thick ends where they were parted from the branches.

In the past, we used to fold tissue paper into cones, so forming nests for the individual fruits which were then packed side by side so that they didn't jostle – we were partly successful in retaining the bloom. These days there is nothing better than the stiffly moulded pâpier-maché container made to hold a half dozen eggs. If they are not the right size, some tissue paper packed around the base of the fruits will help, but on no account should the lids be put on. The long plum or shorter gage stalks should never be covered; they should always be intact and complete. Do not use them to lift the fruits on to the plates but take each plum tenderly at the waistline to lay it on its side. If there is an interval between the times of gathering and showing, the fruits should be put in a cool room, without lifting them from the egg boxes, making sure that wasps cannot get near them. A gauze frame or cage of perforated zinc can be placed over the boxes if the room itself is not wasp proof.

The plate should not have a mound in the middle, as for apples and pears, but it does pay to make a snug nest of crinkled tissue paper in the pan of the plate before lifting the fruits from the boxes and placing them gently on the prepared positions so that they do not roll. Don't let anyone else touch them! Some incautious judge will surely pinch one between finger and thumb, and so mar its appearance for the rest of the show but he will be the first to condemn it if it is marred before he does so.

PEACHES AND NECTARINES*

Peaches are of a higher quality than plums although I personally prefer good gages, no matter the quality of the superior fruit. Peaches are best grown in unheated greenhouses, unless they are to be forced, although quite good crops are often produced outdoors on warm walls, the trees invariably being fan-trained. Actually, they can be trained more easily on walls than can plums, for they have a neater system of bearing. They always produce their crops on the previous year's shoots, therefore the whole aim of the grower is to train the tree in such a way that there is a renewal every year. Mostly the main stem is shortened so that the branches spread sideways instead of being allowed to develop into a top-heavy state.

Nectarines are nothing more nor less than peaches with plain skins instead of the 'felt' that is present on the latter fruit. Some varieties of nectarines are seedlings of peaches and it has never been established which came first, the peach or the nectarine. Generally nectarines are the least hardy, are of smaller sizes, and when compared with their sisters are

* As peaches, nectarines, as well as grapes and other fruits are dealt with in my book *Grow Fruits In Your Greenhouse* (Faber 1970); in this work I merely give those additional hints so necessary for the exhibitor.

less striking – therefore, unless there are special classes for them, they are hardly worth growing just for showing. However, when I have the choice of a peach or a nectarine to eat, the quality being similar, I prefer the nectarine mostly on account of texture and flavour, but that is by the way.

Varieties

There are American varieties of peaches grown on account of earliness and hardiness, mostly outdoors, but for show work we have a range of wonderful English varieties covering the season from early August until early October.

Peregrine is the best known and best of all, and arrives in early August, just right for the shows. Crimson Galande ripens about a fortnight later and is followed by Royal George, then Bellegarde, and at Michaelmas there is Lady Palmerston, and the season finishes with Sea Eagle. All these were raised by a famous English nurseryman named Rivers just over a century ago and they are still supreme.

One of my closest friends of long ago specialised in growing peaches for October shows. He planted them against walls with varying aspects, walls that were fitted with extended overhead glass canopies, and canvases and frames that could be adjusted to the seasonal temperatures. In addition to Lady Palmerston and Sea Eagle, he grew Princess of Wales, Barrington and Violette Hative.

There is also a nectarine named Violette Hative, but for show purposes the one variety that is good for a fortnight in its season, which is early September, is Pine Apple. For earlier shows, Lord Napier arrives in early August, while Elruge comes between the two mentioned. Milton is a late one, while Victoria is last of all.

Both peaches and nectarines are best grown on St Julien A, as for plums.

Cultivation

Chief attentions needed are watering, feeding, thinning, disbudding and control of pests. A winter soaking of the borders is often overlooked, the trees suffering later in consequence. Feeding should be done after the fruits have 'stoned', giving a proprietary fertiliser such as is obtainable from Joseph Bentley, Barrow-on-Humber.

Another task is pollinating the masses of flowers with a brush (we used a rabbit's tail on a bamboo cane). Once the flowers set, thinning begins and is continued gradually until, once they begin to swell, only one fruit to each square foot of the tree front is allowed to mature.

Disbudding begins soon after flowers fade, many of the new leaf shoots being rubbed off, leaving those that are necessary to extend the area of the tree, and the ones that will bear fruit in the next season. Once the fruits have been gathered and the foliage drops, those branches that have borne the crop are pruned to make way for the new shoots which are tied back into position.

Pests

Syringing the boughs and branches daily until fruits begin to ripen should become a routine, so keeping red spider at bay. A little derris in the spray now and again helps against this pest. Aphids can also do a lot of damage unless dealt with, and the derris also controls them. Just when the fruits are getting ripe, ants will often find them; there are proprietary remedies for destroying the nests and it is a good idea to sprinkle some Tugon Ant Killer around the bases of the trees and around entrances to greenhouses. Some gardeners put down a mixture of one part powdered borax and one part castor sugar – this keeps the ants happy during the few days when the fruits are ripening.

Peaches and nectarines have practically no stalk, and have to be removed from the stems very carefully. You can tell when the fruits are almost ripe by pressing very gently with the thumb around the back, close to the diminutive stalk. Then if you place your hand over so that the pressure is spread evenly across the palm, you can twist slowly so that the fruit comes away. Never use the fingers. Some varieties are difficult, and it sometimes pays to cut the shoot off the tree, with the fruit still attached to it. But you have to be very careful when the shoot is removed later, for the fruit will then be softer.

Staging

While it may be advisable to stage the fruit with small pieces of the tree shoots still attached, it is best not to do so unless much damage would be done by removing them. The fruits are best placed on a mounded plate, as for apples, nestling the packing and paper first so that each one can be positioned prominently yet safely.

CHERRIES

There are three types of cherries – sweet, semi-sweet and sour (bitter). Unless your soil and district are favourable it is best to forget about the sweet and semi-sweet varieties, for in order to grow them properly there are all sorts of problems, chief of which is the fact that no sweet cherries are self-fertile. Usually there are no classes for them, but should there be special cherry shows, they will be organised by experts who know more about the subject than the ordinary gardener can ever learn.

However, the sour Morello is a good fruit to grow for home use and for showing at general events and it arrives during August and September most obligingly. The best way to grow this variety is as a fan-trained tree against a west, east, or north wall. It is self-fertile and both grows and bears well. When ripe the fruits are almost black and make a great impression when included in a collection – or it makes a good dish of 'any other fruit'. This variety is generally gathered (if difficult to pull) by snipping off the individual fruits with a pair of scissors, with as much of the stalk as possible.

If you can keep birds away, the best place for the fruits is on the trees until they are required. They will hang for weeks, and improve in colour all the time. The best way to stage them is to place them on a shiny white plate that reflects their brightness.

Other stone fruits, notably almonds, apricots, bullaces, damsons and sloes are seldom staged at general shows. In some instances they are difficult to grow, and in any case they are too insignificant.

20

Other Fruits

While tree fruits may be out of the question for many aspiring horticultural exhibitors, due to lack of room and of time, most of the so-called soft fruits give quick returns, and do not take up as much room nor demand as much time in the growing. They are in general cultivation, as are vegetables, but in order to excel one must take care to prepare the ground, choose the right varieties, and pay attention to specific needs.

Most catalogues and books on fruit growing will tell you that black currants have a different form of growth from the red and the white varieties, and from gooseberries, and will tell you how to prune them. They will also tell you how to cultivate strawberries, raspberries, blackberries, logan-berries, and so on, in a general way – so it is unnecessary to repeat this information here. We are concerned about giving our bushes and plants just that additional fillip to produce for us specimens of their kind that will excel on the show bench.

Taken as a whole, bush fruits need good drainage and plenty of moisture. They suffered terribly from the great drought of 1976, which has set back the production of good stocks for a long time to come. Therefore, when buying for showing one must take the utmost care to obtain new stock that is vigorous and healthy, rather than rashly buying indifferent strains. In times of drought or pestilence, unfortunately, the best stocks are likely to be the first to perish, for we must remember that superior fruits, according to our ideas, are anathema to Nature.

GOOSEBERRIES

At one time gooseberries were given much attention by societies and clubs devoted to their culture, where keeness in getting the largest fruits was a feature. Whether any of these institutions still exist I do not know. They seem to have faded away, and along with them many of the giant varieties. These notes are not intended for such a high degree of competition, but are included to help those who would like to enter these fruits in general shows, in classes amid the roses and sweet peas or other produce during the summer.

Among the best varieties that are still listed in some fruit catalogues are Leveller, New Giant, Careless, Keepsake and Lancer, the last-named being very sizeable when grown well.

The chief needs of gooseberries are deeply worked soil, containing lots of humus-forming manures, and plenty of moisture all the time. In early spring, while the ground is still soaked, a thick layer of rotted manure will keep them going. Rotted garden compost can be an alternative, or another mulch material is sedge peat. If moss peat is used it must be thoroughly soaked first. The chief fertiliser needed is potash, and I find that proprietary dressings formulated for tomatoes are quite useful. If the soil is really moist and the weather is not too hot, slight doses of saltpetre (nitrate of potash) will improve the size of the gooseberries and brighten the foliage.

The way to get those whopper fruits is to prune moderately – not drastically as sometimes advocated – and to start thinning the fruits while they are small, using these for tarts, etc. Continue to thin judiciously, rather than erratically. Syringe the trees frequently. In earlier days, when the fruits were swelling the old growers placed pans of water under the boughs, to give humidity and to stop the fruits splitting.

It is vital to only obtain those stocks that are certified free from viruses. Nothing is more important in all forms of soft fruits than to be sure that they have been propagated from the healthiest parents, proven for quality and size. If your own trees, bushes, or plants are not producing exhibition-quality berries it is most unwise to propagate from them.

On the other hand, if you have a gooseberry or currant bush that produces fruits of outstanding size, you should take the utmost care to keep it healthy and take cuttings from it in the ways prescribed and described in the usual books on fruit growing.

You can grow gooseberries and red and white currants as espaliers quite easily. At one time I had a plantation of them trained to horizontal wires and I obtained super fruits. However, they did not stay healthy for many years, and taken all in all the natural bushes are likely to give the best results, especially over the years.

It is best to keep the fruits on the bushes for as long as possible, up to show time. They may be 'green' or 'ripe' according to the season. They should be gathered carefully, retaining as much of the stalk as possible. I prefer to clip off with scissors, holding the berry tenderly between thumb and finger while doing so. For staging, I place them on a plate lined with a laced paper doily. It stops the fruits rolling, and shows off their colour.

BLACK CURRANTS

Black currants are very popular, and there are frequent competitions for them at shows held during the summer season. The whole secret of getting large bunches of fine fruits is in the preparation of the soil into which humus-forming material, like rotted manure, leafmould and compost, has been worked. This ensures a regular supply of moisture, for that is a most essential feature. The bushes, when growing well, will take fertilisers like fish manures, and give heavy yields.

The books will tell you how to cut the branches down severely in the season of planting, and then in after years to thin out old shoots. Bushes yield their best bunches when three or four years old, and after that, in order to get full-size berries on large well-packed strigs, the old branches that have borne crops should be removed drastically, while ensuring that good new growths are left.

Currants should always be staged as gathered by the bunch. Judges lift them up by the main stalks and critically inspect the size of the berries, and the number on each bunch, and check whether they are of the same quality throughout. 'Tailing off' or gaps in the bunch structure are regarded unfavourably.

In order to ensure good pollination it is best to plant a bush each of three varieties, rather than to have three bushes of the same type, although the latter may be of a super variety. Boskoop Giant, Tor Cross and Wellington XXX can all produce show-standard fruits.

RED AND WHITE CURRANTS
(See also comments under Gooseberries on pp 154–5)

As is well known, red and white currants differ from black-currants in their methods of fruiting, bearing the berries on old shoots as well as young (as do gooseberries) – therefore, the pruning is different. Like gooseberries, they can be grown as trained trees, which black currants cannot. They will thrive in shade, and can be protected from birds more easily. They suffer quickly from lack of water.

The best variety of red currant is Red Lake. If you can get Versailles, it is the best white.

Fruits should always be shown in the bunch, as intact as possible. Placed on a shiny plate that reflects their colour they are startlingly impressive. Another way to stage them, especially if by weight rather than by number of bunches, is to roll up tissue paper into a neat ball, place it firmly in the middle of a plate, and then gently lay the bunches one by one over it to form a mound, taking care to put the best bunches on top, for these are the ones that will be examined.

STRAWBERRIES

At most summer shows there are classes for strawberries, stipulating a certain number of fruits. The best fruits are obtained from one-year-old plants, having been propagated from runners the previous season. By careful selection it is possible to have one's own strain. When this fruit was afflicted with diseases that nearly put it out of cultivation, before the clone system of increase was practised, I managed to keep my stocks going by treating them as annuals.

Runners were taken off the best plants each summer immediately after flowering, while the rest were allowed to bear as many fruits as possible. Once the season was over, the cropped plants and those from which runners had been taken were all burned. However, this is unnecessary now if clean stocks are obtained from certificated stocks – which should always be the case, unless you grow your own.

Expert growers still cultivate the queen of all strawberries – Royal Sovereign. But, for the average gardener, the very best variety to grow, either for home consumption or for showing, is Red Gauntlet. Quite often it will produce a second crop in late summer, and one can sometimes find enough fruits to stage at the general show – in the class for any other fruit.

When gathering for showing, I like to pick them with as much stalk as possible and enclose each one in a leaf, placing them side by side in a shallow box so that they do not move in transit. Size, ripeness (but not over-ripeness), evenness and colour are all considerations. As with gooseberries, I like to place them on a plate, the middle of which is covered with a doily – this stops them rolling.

RASPBERRIES, LOGANBERRIES AND BLACKBERRIES

Generally, raspberries and the allied loganberries, etc, grow in light soils containing plenty of leafmould. Peat and compost are also good conditioners, while mulching does much towards producing large juicy berries that will not deteriorate too quickly, the bug bear of showing these fruits.

Unless you are an expert, and have the best facilities for growing raspberries, the best variety is Malling Exploit, the berries being large and keeping firm. An alternative is Lloyd George, but there are so many bad stocks about that it is often difficult to get good virus-free stocks or keep them free from all sorts of troubles.

The fruits are always gathered with the stalks complete for show purposes. I pick them off by nipping through the stalk with finger and thumbnail, carefully putting each berry on an apple leaf, at the same time placing the latter in a flat box as close as possible to others so that they fill the base, keep steady, and do not jostle in transit. It always pays to take many more along than you actually need so that only the freshest are laid out direct upon the doily covering the plate.

There are several diseases and pests that attack raspberries, blackberries and loganberries. One of the latter is the beetle that causes maggots inside the fruits. Both derris and malathion control this bother if spraying or dusting is carried out soon after the flowers have faded, and before the fruit's swell to perfection.

Quite often, one can put on a 'dish' of blackberries, or logan-berries, at the autumn shows. Raspberries are seldom in season at this time, either being too early or too late.

MELONS

Quite often a melon will take the first prize at the summer shows in the 'any other fruit' class. It is, in the estimation of the *Horticultural Show Handbook* (see p. 22), a 20-pointer, compared with gooseberries that are merely 8-pointers, as are red and white currants, while black currants are 12-pointers. Whereas I, as a judge, would give the award to a perfect dish of any of these bush fruits rather than to a miserly melon, there are others who, knowing these points values, would favour the melon.

When all is said and done, a melon is only a glorified cucumber, especially if it is one of the so-called hardy varieties grown in a cold frame. On the other hand, there are some glorious fruits of superior quality that have red or green flesh; these need warmth and much attention to bring them to perfection. Then we have the cantaloups that thrive well in a hot-bed within a frame.

In growing methods, the chief mistake is to make too rich a bed for the plants to grow in. Soil taken from the garden where it was manured for a previous crop will do, or if loam can be obtained some well-decayed manure can be added along with bonemeal. A dusting of lime is necessary. The hothouse melons need warmth and a humid atmosphere. They should never be allowed to become dry or they will split.

Timing is an important item. To get a fruit, or fruits, ripe on the right day demands careful planning. Those grown in heat will mature about three months from sowing, while the frame varieties need from sixteen to twenty weeks, depending upon variety, weather and aspect.

Training melon plants involves pinching back. Instead of nipping out the growing tip of the plant when the first supporting wire is reached (if in the greenhouse), the plant is allowed to grow until it gets to the top wire and then the tip is pinched out. The subsequent side-growths are trained outwards along the wires until flowers and tiny fruits have formed, and then the tips of the shoots are nipped out.

The next thing is fertilisation. The female flowers with their embryo fruits behind them must be fertilised, or they will not develop. This is done by picking off a male flower and applying the pollen-laden anthers to the stigmas of the female. If the flowers 'take', the miniature fruits quickly begin to swell.

If more than one fruit is needed on a plant, care has to be taken to ensure that there are at least four female flowers in an equal state of development. It is best to have them at this stage before doing the pollination. If all four 'take', you get four melons. However, for showing purposes, you then remove the weakest three out of the four, so that all nourishment goes into the one remaining.

Melons must be grown quickly to be good. It should not take more than four months before your chosen specimen is ripe. When growing on a trellis in the greenhouse, it has to be supported by placing under it a net cradle. When the fruit is becoming sizeable, the skin begins to develop mysterious markings that are the beginning of a process known as 'netting'. This is most pronounced in the hothouse varieties.

When the fruits have reached maturity they begin to change colour and this is a sign that watering should be gradually withheld. The foliage then yellows and the fruit begins to smell very 'melon-ish'. To test for ripeness, you push your thumb flatly on the old flower scar and when this 'gives' slightly it is time to sever the fruit from the vine, about an inch from the neck. I like to leave the fruit in the net hammock for a day or so before removing it to a cool shed where it can ripen at leisure, and I then hope that it will be in good condition on the day of the show. The best way to stage is to sit the fruit stalk uppermost on a plate that has been decorated with coloured vine leaves.

I have purposely dealt with the melon in some detail because much of the information is not reiterated in general books, although they will tell you about some of its diseases. Another reason for discussing melons is that there are no years of waiting before positive results begin – it is the quickest of all fruits to grow from a seed, and one is either very successful or one fails. You will most likely be successful, if you follow my methods.

Still another reason for growing melons for show is that, if you stage collections, they are among the highest pointers, only being equalled by dessert apples, dessert pears, peaches, nectarines, pineapples and the choicest of grapes.

GRAPES

There are many other fruits that cannot be considered because they are so seldom grown, and when they are, they do not add much to a showman's glory or rewards. However, grape vines are to be found in many gardens, ranging from the muscats in the greenhouses down to the small varieties that grow outdoors on walls. The commonest is Black Hamburg. There are plenty of sources of information regarding cultivation and all I will do here is reveal how to stage them to the best effect.

Although it is many years since I staged grapes, I have still the original box in which were carried four bunches upon their respective stands. Each stand consisted of a board the size of a piece of foolscap paper, held at a slope by a bracket, after the manner of photographs on the sideboard. Each one was faced with a layer of cotton wool and this in turn was covered with a few sheets of clean tissue paper fixed with drawing pins at the back. Above the bracket at the back was placed a small hook to hold a strong piece of raffia at the other end of which was the bunch of grapes, suspended over the front of the board. The wooden box and the brackets were made by an estate carpenter so that they fitted exactly, and when the lid was closed there was no movement whatsoever inside. The only thing that would upset the bunches would be to tilt the box the wrong side up. If only one or two bunches were to be taken to a show, all four stands were fitted in so that there would be no movement.

The whole object of this exercise was to get those bunches on to the exhibition table without in any way brushing off the natural bloom with which all grapes are endowed.

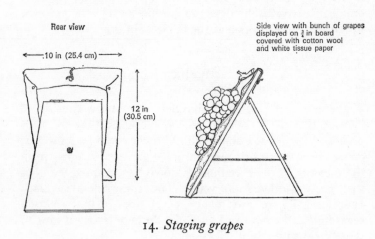

Rear view

←—:10 in (25.4 cm) ——→

12 in
(30.5 cm)

Side view with bunch of grapes
displayed on ¾ in board
covered with cotton wool
and white tissue paper

14. *Staging grapes*

Appendix: Garden Literature

The number of gardening books is legion. An aspiring competitor who strives to achieve his ambitions by reading everything would have no time to attend to his plants; he must therefore be very selective and only consult those works that will be helpful in the most practical ways. These can include not only books, but also booklets issued by authorities such as the Ministry of Agriculture, the Department of Environment and the Royal Horticultural Society, seed catalogues or pamphlets put out by firms who have products to sell. I have a fairly extensive library and piles of advertising leaflets and so on, a few of which I study more than the rest, knowing that they will give me the information I need, frequently providing reassurance and sometimes reminding me of matters I have forgotten.

One book I often refer to is *In Your Garden With Percy Thrower* (Hamlyn). Most of its pages are filled with week-by-week reminders of what to do in the vegetable plot, the flower borders, and the greenhouse. While it would be foolish to carry out all these tasks within the particular times suggested, the book is a sound general guide to what to do as the days pass, and it saves me trying to remember everything.

Throughout the years, I've worn out three copies of *Sanders Encyclopaedia of Gardening* (Collingridge). Whenever in doubt about the name of a tree, or plant, and the sort of cultivation it needs, the answer is in that much condensed comprehensive work. It was first compiled in 1895 by a working gardener who eventually became the editor of a gardening journal. Revised editions appear from time to time.

Catalogues are essential aids to showing. Among those I study avidly every winter are those of Suttons Seeds Ltd, Torquay; Dobies Seeds, Chester; Unwins, Histon, Cambridgeshire; Thompson & Morgan, Ipswich, Suffolk; and Marshall & Co., Wisbech, Cambridgeshire. By studying these and others available it is possible to keep up-to-date on all the newest varieties of vegetables and annual flowers and, by comparing one with another, to get winning ideas of what to choose and grow. The old trusted varieties should be the mainstay, but one must be prepared to try out anything that seems to be an advancement.

There are comparatively few comprehensive fruit catalogues available. Unfortunately, owing to the times in which we live, many of the old quality fruits are going out of cultivation, and lists are much of a muchness within a limited range. However, one catalogue that I do treasure is that of John Scott and Co., the Royal Nurseries, Marriot, Somerset, which is a great deal better than some theoretical works on the subject. Many varieties of apples are listed, and valuable information given about each. Rivers and Son, Sawbridgeworth, Herts, are also very helpful.

There are also small firms specialising in particular crops, such as onions, or leeks, or potatoes. These are generally advertised in the weekly gardening newspaper *Garden News*. This journal will give more help, particularly to the beginner at showing, than any other source of periodical information. At the same time, it is much a matter of personal judgement regarding the value of what you find advertised and of which expert advice to follow. And here, I offer a word of warning. Quite often, extensive advertisers in periodicals do not always supply good plants. The best sources for reliable varieties are small local nurseries or reputable garden centres where you can see before you buy, and carry the plants home without damage. Plants sent by post can suffer greatly.

A considerable amount of free literature on fertilisers is put out by the big companies. This can be very helpful indeed if we read the advertising matter with a degree of discretion, and study the basic ingredients of the branded products. Experience brings assurance in this matter. Tentative trials of 'magical formulae' will reveal the real values.

If you are tempted by the descriptive blurbs sent out by manufacturers of garden machinery, the surest way to find out is to insist upon a trial in your own garden, with yourself at the controls. Whether machinery helps the aspiring showman very much is a moot point; so much depends upon the size of the garden and the type of soil. Generally, the most efficient cultivators are too substantial for moving around in a small area, while the ones that are manageable do not dig deep enough.

VEGETABLES

In recent times many books about the cultivation of vegetables have been published. Very few are written by 'horny-handed' gardeners, and many are but re-hashed bits of information superficially collected by journalists. I have yet to read anything to supersede an old copy of *The Profitable Culture of Vegetables* by Thomas Smith (Longmans Green), which has only been reprinted infrequently. It has a market garden slant, but the information can be applied to the amateur's garden, especially if the reader intends to be a successful exhibitor.

For those who do not like to use chemical fertilisers or pesticides, the more modern works of Mr L. D. Hills are those of a practical grower who firmly believes in organic methods and I recommend his *Down to Earth Fruit and Vegetable Growing* (Faber).

For brevity and clear presentation of information charts, tables and pictures, there are two useful publication. One is *The Vegetable Garden Displayed* (RHS) and the other *Vegetable Plotter* by Dr D. G. Hessayon (Pan Britannica Industries). This second is helpful to the exhibitor in that it gives the names of the best varieties for showing and contains other useful items such as how long it takes seeds to germinate, and also gives records of champion vegetables that have been grown.

There are books available regarding the special cultivation of certain vegetables, one popular subject being tomatoes. My own knowledge comes from years of practical experience so I have not needed to study any of these books, but if one is unfamiliar with the various methods of growing tomatoes, or any other crop, such works are well worth consulting, the more so if one's first attempts have not been entirely successful. Typical of such books is the paperback *Tomatoes for Everyone* by F. W. Allerton (Faber).

FRUIT

It has been impossible in this book to include much, let alone all, there is to know about the cultivation of fruit, for in reality one could write a dozen books about the various kinds. Rather than attempting to give detailed advice, I have merely dwelt upon the arts of preparing and staging as practised through the years.

A book I've consulted more than any other is *Tree Fruit Growing* by Raymond Bush (RHS and Penguin), dealing as it does with the propagation, planting and general management of apples, pears, plums, peaches and nectarines, medlars, apricots, figs and so on. There is a host of things to learn about them all, ranging from the kinds of stocks to the different diseases, and problems of cross-pollination.

Training and pruning play very important parts in the successful cultivation of most tree fruits and, besides Raymond Bush's excellent general book, there are others well worth studying, if one aspires to become a local authority on this one aspect of a vast subject. Such a work is *Pruning Apple Trees* by C. R. Thompson (Faber).

Earlier in my long career I took an intense interest in the culture of indoor fruits and wrote a book about it called *Grow Fruit In Your Greenhouse* (Faber), which I am pleased to say was well received by many experts as well as by amateurs. It deals with the growing of grapes, peaches and nectarines, figs and melons. I am aware that others have since been written, but I have no personal experience of them.

I would recommend to anyone who wants to know more about strawberries, raspberries, gooseberries, currants and blackberries *Soft Fruit Growing* by E. G. Gilbert (RHS and Penguin). This, together with the literature dispensed by Ken Muir, the berried-fruit specialist, of Honeypot Fruit Farm, Clacton-on-Sea, Essex, should enable an absorbing facet of horticulture to be tackled quite confidently. *The Fruit Garden Displayed* (RHS) is also recommended.

ROSES AND OTHER FLOWERS

There are many excellent books about roses. One that I frequently delve into is *Roses* by Leonard Hollis (Collingridge) and another is *Rose Growing Complete* by E. B. Le Grice (Faber). When I'm seeking particular advice on cultivation, checking up on ways to cope with pests and diseases, or considering varieties to plant or recommend, the advice of two such experts charts the course of action I shall take.

If I wanted to specialise in the showing of roses I would be a member of The Royal National Rose Society, Bone Hill, St Albans, Hertfordshire, in order to get every issue of *The Rose Annual*. No need then to bother about the addresses of the specialists for practically all of them have advertisements in that publication.

Generally, in local shows, there are classes for collections of flowers, such as perennials, hardy annuals, etc. as well as for separate subjects like chrysanthemums, dahlias, or pot begonias. Much help can be obtained by reading specialist books studying catalogues and reading literature issued by societies devoted to the welfare of the respective genera. There are specialist societies for almost all flowers grown for show. In some instances their addresses are far less permanent than that of The Royal National Rose Society. Practically all their officials act in an honorary capacity and the headquarters is often the private address of the secretary, so it is best to send an enquiry with a stamped addressed envelope to the Royal Horticultural Society, Vincent Square, London SW1P 2PE, or to a firm specializing in the plant concerned, in order to get up-to-date information.

To my knowledge there are societies devoted to the welfare of alpines, camellias, carnations, chrysanthemums, dahlias, delphiniums, ferns, fuchsias, gladioli, irises, pansies and sweet peas; all on a national level. In addition there are innumerable local specialist societies as well as the general district organisations that exist in every town, and in the majority of villages. The larger societies send out very helpful literature and impressive, colourful annuals, such as those issued by The Delphinium Society and The National Sweet Pea Society. If you wish to develop an intense interest in any flower it is most advisable to become a member of the organisation involved. Not only is the reading matter invaluable, but also you have at your elbow the addresses from which to obtain your stock plants.

Some of the specialist firms of international repute issue books or pamphlets written by the principals, and these give very reliable advice. For example, Blackmore and Langdon of Pensfold, Bristol, publish cultural booklets about begonias, delphiniums and polyanthuses. This firm excels in the production of these three flowers.

PESTS AND DISEASES

Practically everything we grow is, unfortunately, subject to attack by all sorts of parasites. When things go wrong we seek ways and means to put them right. Some rush unreservedly to suppliers of chemical antidotes, and others strive to do things without such recourse, attempting to control garden enemies by means of 'safe' insecticides and fungicides. In this connection, *Pest Control Without Poisons* published by The Henry Doubleday Research Association, Bocking, Essex, will be more acceptable than the many pamphlets issued by manufacturers of very potent chemicals.

While I respect the various 'muck and mystery' schools, I confess that, like the overwhelming majority of market growers and gardeners, I do resort to chemicals when it is deemed essential. But I endeavour to learn about all the consequences of whatever action I take before doing so.

Free literature issued by manufacturers, particularly Murphy, Pan Britannica Industries, Fisons and ICI is very helpful in determining the nature of the insects, fungi, or virus bothers. In some instances, the charts depict the various main troubles so that we can rcognise them. They also, quite understandably, tell us which of the antidotes to use, quoting their brand names. But practically every brand name covers the product container brightly, while in very small lettering is given the character of the actual contents, which will either be a straight chemical, or a mixture of two or more. Before using any brand I learn about the after effects of the various poisons by studying *Approved Products for Farmers and Growers*, a book of considerable dimensions, published annually by the Ministry of Agriculture. It gives a wealth of information regarding the practical application of acaricides, fungicides, insecticides, molluscicides, herbicides and dessicants. Furthermore, we are told which of the products persist, and those that disperse quickly. To give one example, there are many brands of sprays, dusts or smokes that contain HCH (or BHC), also known as lindane, or gamma-HCH, to kill ants, earwigs, flea beetles, leatherjackets, etc. For some crops it is awful stuff, tainting roots such as carrots, and we are advised in this book not to plant potatoes for at least 18 months after application.

Actually, everything used to kill pests must perforce be a poison, if only to the thing it is intended to annihilate. So-called non-poisonous insecticide like derris is deadly to fish and to bees. Reluctantly, we must control the spread of pests and diseases, just as our own health is guarded by the medical profession. To learn by referring when necessary to that annual book saves both expense and the destruction of not only some of the crops, but of harmless creatures as well.

Finally, during my many years both as a competitor and a judge, I have met very successful countrymen at shows, even in London, who could not read. They have gained their knowledge purely by working for their fathers, or other much experienced gardeners, and heeding everything they hear, using their own powers of shrewdness and ability to succeed in whatever they set out to do. They are a fast-fading race. A lot of what I've written down in this book I learned from such men. I find it impossible to remember how I came to acquire all I know, whether it is from hearsay, or magazines or books. I am still learning from all these sources.

Index

171